Wicked 46
A Pennsylvania Haunting

Wicked 46
A Pennsylvania Haunting

by Dave Spinks and David Weatherly

Edited by Jerry Hajewski

Cover art by Gerald Vance
AdVANCEd Creations

Layout: SMAK
smakgraphics.com

© 2016, Revised Edition © 2021

All rights reserved.

No part of this publication may be reproduced or transmitted in any form, or by any means, mechanical or electronic, including photocopying and recording, or by any information storage and retrieval system, without permission in writing from the author or publisher (except by a reviewer, who may quote brief passages in articles or reviews).

ISBN: 978-1-945950-27-8

EERIE LIGHTS

Eerie Lights Publishing
Eerielightspublishing.com

Also from Eerie Lights Publishing:

By Dave Spinks

West Virginia Bigfoot

Real West Virginia Hauntings Vol 1

By David Weatherly

Strange Intruders
Eerie Companions:

A History of Haunted Dolls

Monsters of the Last Frontier:
Cryptids & Legends of Alaska

Monsters at the Crossroads:
Cryptids & Legends of Indiana

Paranormal Files West Virginia
by David Weatherly, Ross Allison, and Dave Spinks

Dedication

This book is dedicated First and Foremost, to my Mom, you are truly missed. To my family, you are my everything. And to all my friends and fans who support what I do.

~ Dave Spinks

To those who dare the unknown.

~ David Weatherly

Table of Contents

Introduction — *David Weatherly* — 1

A Brief History of the Welles House — *David Weatherly* — 5

My Start in the Paranormal — *Dave Spinks* — 17

Disclaimer — *Dave Spinks* — 21

The Investigative Journal of Dave Spinks — 23

Testimonials — 131

Bambi — 131

Norene — 133

An Unsettled Valley — *David Weatherly* — 137

Aftermath — *Dave Spinks* — 147

About the Authors — 153

Introduction
David Weatherly

I routinely travel to what many consider the creepiest locations in the world. Dark, haunted spots with reputations as grim as their often-dilapidated conditions. Each of these places has its own unique character. Some are simply repositories of long forgotten stories, some, storehouses of grand memories, and others…well, others are different.

There are some places that are so disturbed, so unsettling, that you can feel the darkness scratching against you as if "something" wants to get inside you, inside your mind, your body, and inside your soul.

These are the places that have an unnatural presence, as if something has taken up residence within and wants to feed.

My friend Dave Spinks and I stood on the porch of a house in a darkened neighborhood in Wilkes-Barre, Pennsylvania. Although it was early evening, most of the surrounding houses had little or no lights on. There were few streetlights, and to top off the scene, it had started to storm, so rain was coming down quickly, the wind throwing drops against us even as we stood under cover.

Seconds after mounting the steps, we both heard a loud "boom" from within the house, just inside the front door, as if something had been thrown down a flight of steps. It was startling, but considering the house, it was not completely unexpected.

Something knew we were there, and Dave believed the house itself knew he had returned. He was uneasy, and I can tell you, it's not a normal condition for Dave Spinks. Dave is former military, and after his service, he spent years working for the Department of Justice, guarding and transporting the worst criminals and terrorists alive. When he retired from those roles, he threw himself full time into his passion, pursuing the paranormal.

Just like me, Dave's been in some of the creepiest places you can imagine, and it's hard for him to get rattled. But this place, this place was one of those different ones that I mentioned. You see, the house at 46 South Welles Street has a long history of disturbing reports. Poltergeist-like activity, stories of a demonic presence, and numerous strange deaths are merely a fraction of the events that have taken place behind the walls of what appears, from the outside, to be a normal, neighborhood home.

It's also the location where Dave Spinks undertook one of the most intensive investigations of his career. And his experiences in the Welles house changed him.

Permanently.

Day after day, night after night, he stayed in the home with a few fellow investigators, using every tool at their disposal to try to uncover answers about the location's disturbing past and the phenomena that was being reported from the place.

But getting answers from any haunting, especially a negative location, is no easy task. Despite the vast range of equipment now available to paranormal investigators, it is still a challenge to find a collective grouping of evidence that creates a solid trail to answers and solutions.

It is, for all intents and purposes, like trying to put together a massive, complex puzzle, without any knowledge of what the final picture should be.

Equipment, at its best, gives readings on various aspects of the environment being investigated. Temperature, EMF, movement, and sound all are things that can be tracked and recorded using various types of paranormal devices. But haunted locations are notorious for causing difficulties with physical equipment. Readings can be erratic and inconsistent, and at times equipment can go completely haywire. This is, of course, in and of itself quite interesting, but at the same time it adds another level of difficulty to the collection of evidence.

Another aspect of technology that investigators widely use are various instruments to allow communication with whoever, or whatever, may be on the other side. From age old talking boards to modern hacked radios, people have been trying to make contact with spirits as far back in history as you can imagine time. Modern devices allow spirits and entities a "voice" to send information through. Sometimes those voices and their messages are quite disturbing.

Extremely negative locations add a whole different layer of difficulty to investigation, and if a negative entity is present or active, even the human senses can become overwhelmed and confused as these beings attempt to manipulate and coerce those who have stepped into their domain. Imagine attempting to investigate a location and having to question your own perceptions, or worse, your own sanity.

I sometimes think exploring the supernatural should come with a warning. As the old saying goes, "enter at your own risk," for if you do choose to enter such spaces, there's no telling what consequences will lie ahead and what the ongoing effects may be.

Negative places like the Welles house can take a toll on one's life and spirit. Dave walked away, not an easy task, battered and scarred by the experience, but wiser and ultimately stronger for having come through the crucible of what lay inside the home. But he paid a price.

You are about to read his story and as you do, bear in mind, Dave continues to be haunted by the events that took place at the Welles house. He has chosen to share his experience in hopes that others will understand the paranormal is not a game, not an entertainment to be taken lightly, but a serious path with many potential pitfalls.

A Brief History of the Welles House

David Weatherly

"It's haunted. It's definitely haunted. Haunting phenomenon has definitely taken place here. Vibrations still remain here. I can feel them."

So declared renowned demonologist Ed Warren as he and his wife Lorraine stood in front of the house at 46 South Welles Street in Wilkes-Barre, Pennsylvania.

The year was 1980 and the couple were in town during a lecture tour. On March 3 they stopped by the infamous Welles house to take a look and speak with reporter Mark L. Hoffman, staff writer from the *Times Leader*.

For some unreported reason, the couple were not allowed to enter the home, but Lorraine sat down on the side porch and gathered herself to relay some of the impressions she picked up about the house:

"I sense terrible despair. The effect on people who lived in this house was very, very negative. There were separations, personality changes. People who lived here were driven to self-destruction of the body through drugs, alcohol, even suicide."

Hoffman's article, titled *"Ghost hunter says there's spirits in Heights house,"* detailed the Warrens' visit and was one of many in a series of pieces written about the home in local papers.

The Welles house had previously been featured in the *Times Leader* by writer Keith Schneider, who penned an article in 1979 titled *"Wilkes-Barre's 'Amityville Horror' isn't just a Halloween Joke."*

Appropriately, the article was published on October 31.

The Welles house is in the "Heights" section of the city, an area expanded after the Civil War with streets named after prominent figures from the period. Lincoln and Grant both have nearby streets named after them, and Welles Street itself is named after former Secretary of the Navy, Gideon Welles.

The land on Welles Street was originally one large piece of property purchased by industrialist Augustus C. Laning in the mid-1800s. Odd deaths cropped up early in the property's history. Lightning struck a barn on the property and led to a fire. Not only were horses killed, but in a freak twist, Laning's nephew, who was working with the horses, was trapped in the barn beneath the carcass of a horse and he also perished.

The incident was covered in the typical, somewhat graphic style of the period in the *Wilkes-Barre Times* under the banner: *"Met A Shocking Death. Harry Laning Pinned Under a Horse and Is Burned to Death."* The article reports:

"The young man was 23 years old, a son of Augustus Laning, a well-known and prosperous farmer of Ross township.

"The young man was working with a team of horses on the farm and when the storm came up, he drove to the barn and began to unharness the horses. While engaged in that work a terrific bolt of lightning struck the barn, killing both horses. It seems that young Laning was not injured by the lightning, but one of the horses fell on him, pinning him to the ground. He was unable to escape, and the barn burned about him like a huge funeral pyre, burning him to a crisp.

"The young man's father and other farm hands rushed to the barn when they saw it in flames, but they were unable to rescue the unfortunate young man, who could be seen in the fiery furnace struggling to free himself from under the horse."

According to the article, the group watched as the injured man, trapped by the weight of the horse, gave up his fight and crawled under the carcass of the animal until he perished. His remains were later retrieved and carried to his home.

The elder Laning himself lost his fortune in another fire-related incident when his factories burned to the ground. He passed away in 1875 and the property was divided, with the portion that would become the infamous number 46 going to one B.R. Honeywell.

Ownership of the home changed hands numerous times into the early 1900s. The property was frequently used as a rental home, but as the years wore on, many tenants didn't stay in the house very long. On three occasions, the home ended up as part of a sheriff's sale. The area itself became more troubled as the economic fortunes of Wilkes-Barre faded, and the Heights was no longer considered the "in" place to be.

As the years wore on, disturbing stories came from the Welles house. Reportedly, a lot of the people who live in the home sank into depression, alcoholism, and drug abuse. Families split, there was financial ruin, health issues, and accidents. Several of the home's residents became suicidal, and no one wanted to visit the families who did try to live in the Welles house. Friends and relatives would come by, but after a visit or two, they found the place was simply too unsettling to remain even for a brief visit.

As families came and went, the stories increased and seemed to become stranger and stranger. A young girl "floated" down the stairs; a pregnant woman thought her baby was cursed to be a devil; and lonely people sat in the dark basement for hours talking to someone, or something, that no one else could see.

Worse still, there were accounts of odd deaths and suicides connected to the home. News reports state that previous residents committed suicide in the house in 1940 and 1950.

One report published in the *Times Leader* quoted a professor of psychology from Wilkes College, who stated he remembered stories of hauntings at the Welles house during the days of the Great Depression when he was a boy of 13-17 years of age. The professor, Joseph Kanner, stated:

"When I was growing up, that house was empty for most of the time. The neighbors said it was haunted. We would walk by there as kids and neighbors would yell to us to stay away from there. There always was something unusual about that house."

As families came and went, stories grew about strange events occurring within the home. In the 1970s the tales escalated, and by the latter part of the decade the stories became public, with several newspaper reports detailing incidents taking place at the haunted

Welles house.

Much of the home's modern lore seems to have arisen with a family first called the "Johnsons" in news reports. The family later came out in the open and their real name was revealed to be Bennett.

Walker Bennett and his family lived in the home briefly but vacated it suddenly. Walker told news reporters that he believed the home was Wilkes-Barre's own version of the "Amityville Horror" house.

Bennett claimed he had seen apparitions of several different people at the house, including a young girl in a nightgown and a well-dressed man with a cane who knocked at the door. These incidents were documented in the initial article about the bizarre incidents at the home that appeared in the *Times Leader* in its Halloween 1979 edition.

Bear in mind this story refers to the family as the "Johnsons" since they had requested anonymity during the early stages of reports.

Among the "Johnsons'" claims were that they were being paid nightly visits by a "well-dressed phantom who disappeared before their eyes." They also reported witnessing a young girl who would walk through closed doors, and they heard shrieks, moans, and unexplained crying that seemed to come from both the attic and within the walls of the house.

"First it was scratching and knocking sounds at the front door." Then, Johnson says, he'd open the door and see a human-like figure so translucent the streetlights shined through it. He said the figure resembled a well-dressed man in a dark suit carrying a cane. The figure would disappear seconds after the front door opened.

"I remember seeing a smile on the face," Johnson says with a shudder. "It was crooked and vicious."

The ghostly visitations were just the beginning of the incidents at the home. The following week, a disgusting stench developed in the kitchen from somewhere behind the cabinets. The man reported that the stench smelled like decay, as if something had died in the room. He tore the wall down trying to find the source but discovered nothing to explain the foul odor.

The family reached out to members of the parapsychology field for help, and nationally renowned parapsychologist Mary Pascerella became involved. Pascerella had worked on the Amityville case and agreed to investigate the Welles house, but not until the family recorded the sounds they were hearing. Pascerella wanted to be sure the incidents were not related to natural causes.

The family followed the directions and found the activity increased once they began their efforts to capture it on recordings. They reported the increase in a range of sounds, from banging and shrieking to disembodied voices. There were crashing sounds from the kitchen that sounded like dishes breaking, and most unsettling, the sound of a baby crying even though there was no baby in the home. They reported this to Pascerella who agreed to pay the family a visit and investigate the location. According to the *Times Leader*:

"When Pascerella arrived she immediately felt the presence of something supernatural. Something so strong that she counseled Johnson to conduct a historical check of the house and the area. Whatever it was, she said before she left, it must be pacified, or the house should be demolished."

In the news article, the family also mentioned a weird, antique doll that appeared one morning from nowhere amongst the youngest daughter's toys. None of the other family members had given the girl the doll, and they reported that the thing was rather creepy in appearance.

"I'll never forget that doll. Looking at it made you shiver. The doll was naked, its body cracked with age. The face was as soft as a baby's, however, and its lips were painted a glowing red. The eyes were piercing and bitter."

One of the most well-known stories associated with the Welles house came from Walker Bennett's time. Bennett reported witnessing his daughter trip at the top of a flight of stairs, but instead of plummeting down the steps, she floated in slow motion through the air, and landed at the bottom of the steps without so much as a scratch on her.

Oddly, the incident repeated itself a month later, and this time Bennett's wife witnessed the strange occurrence.

Amid the apparitions and creepy sounds resonating around the home, the Bennetts began to experience another disturbing phenomenon; pools of blood started to manifest on the walls in the living room.

Walker Bennett became so disturbed by the strange sounds

echoing from the home he knocked down one of the walls in the back bedroom in an attempt to find the source of the disturbances. What he found were not answers, but more questions. Tucked inside the wall was a small tin box. Opening it, Bennett discovered an assortment of items; a human molar and chicken bones, all tied together with red ribbon in the form of a cross.

Bennett believed the items were related to black magic and connected to a rumored voodoo curse that legend said had been placed against Augustus C. Laning, the first owner of the property. Bennett also reported he had found an old photograph in the house that he believed to be of Laning.

The Bennetts became more and more unsettled while trying to remain in the home. They decided to have the house cleansed and called in Reverend McGahagan of the Holy Trinity Rectory in Wilkes-Barre to bless the house and hopefully exorcise whatever was tormenting the family. The blessing, however, didn't seem to have much effect, and the activity continued, even escalating to some degree.

The final straw for the family came one night in March 1978. They were awakened by what they first thought was the loud crashing of thunder. Walker got up and looked outside only to find the skies were clear and there was no storm.

Other sounds quickly began to surround them. Pounding footsteps echoed from the attic. The front door started shaking and rattling as if someone was attempting to enter; there was the sound of dishes crashing in the kitchen; and perhaps the most disturbing manifestation, the family heard the cry of a child coming from behind the very walls of the home.

Walker Bennett had reached his limit. He took his family out that night, leaving behind all their belongings, including a range of high-end electronic equipment. They wanted nothing else to do with the haunted Welles house.

Even the priest the family had called on, Reverend McGahagan, agreed with their departure, stating: "It is most imperative for them to vacate the premises for their own psychological well-being."

Bennett's comments about his time in the house would later be echoed by other stories of the home's tormented residents: "There was a period just before we left when hanging myself didn't look so bad,"

Bennett reports.

An article in the *Times Leader* reported that Bennett confessed to: "a severe drinking problem brought on by experiences at the house, chain-smoking cigarettes and regularly under-going professional counseling."

So, what in the world is lurking within the walls of the house at 46 South Welles Street?

It's a question that has intrigued investigators for years, starting with luminaries such as Ed and Lorraine Warren, Mary Pascerella, and in recent years a host of paranormal teams and individual researchers who have visited and investigated the home.

Well-known paranormal investigator John Zaffis, is of the opinion that the house is most certainly haunted stating: "There is definitely paranormal activity that transpires in the [Welles] house. It has that heavy feeling you associate with haunted environments."

Deadline Paranormal conducted an investigation of the site in 2013. The investigation was covered by reporter Elizabeth Skrapits of the local *Citizen Voice*. She writes: "Jim Fazzi and Tony Piontkowski, the veteran law enforcement officers who co-founded Deadline Paranormal, say the house dates back to the Civil War era and has a history of unexplained phenomena. Their goal is to rule out things with simple explanations and look further into those without them.

"The house was built around 1860 by Augustus C. Laning— 'He's the guy they think might be here,' Fazzi said, noting that one of the residents saw an apparition of a well-dressed man knocking on the door. 'In the 1940s and 1950s, there were two suicides in the house,' Fazzi said."

Skrapits spoke with Stacey Evans, whose mother Katherine "Kaye" Watkins had passed away, leaving her the house. She voiced concern over the salability of the home due to its ghostly reputation. With the house full of ghost hunters, Evans commented that her mother wouldn't like all the strangers in her home, noting that her mother would likely be "rolling over in her grave" due to the intrusion.

Evans believes her mother's spirit is still in the home, a belief echoed by her aunt, Judy Benson: "She never wanted to leave this house, really, so she's probably still there, I believe she's there. She needs to move on, and she doesn't want to move on. She has unfinished business."

Deadline Paranormal's Fazzi went on to recount some of the other popular stories associated with the home and stated that his team believed the home was an active haunting and that the source could be dark in nature. "It could be hexed; it could be something from the suicides hanging around."

Before the team had even finished setting up all their equipment, investigators got a hit. A video camera set up in the basement captured an elongated, white object floating through the darkness. The paper described the anomaly as looking "something like an electric eel."

As the night wore on, members of Deadline Paranormal reported several other incidents, including more light anomalies and unexplained sounds. According to the team's online report, whenever investigators were in the dining room, there would be increased activity in the basement. (Access to the basement is via the kitchen, just off the dining room.) If members stepped out of the area, the activity would cease. Additionally, two team members reported seeing a shadow figure in the kitchen doorway.

Another paranormal group, the Valley Shadow-walkers, investigated the Welles house in the spring of 2013. Writing a guest piece for the *Wilkes-Barre Independent Gazette* on April 13, team member TD covered the team's experience in the home as well as some of the incidents that occurred during their investigation:

"Not long ago we were talking to a good friend, Betsy Summers. Well known in local political circles, Ms. Summers had told us previously about this 'haunted house' she was taking care of. Betsy told us that she heard someone walking around on the floor above her when no one was home and that a former resident moved out of a bedroom because something used to shake the bed. She had heard stories of a suicide taking place in the home."

According to the report, activity started even during the team's initial walkthrough of the home:

"I decided to have a look at the upstairs level. Ascending the stairs to the second floor, this investigator witnessed a bright flash of light like a tiny flashbulb at the top of the stairs, near the ceiling, and without the aid of any equipment."

The team also reported a high electromagnetic field halfway up the stairs. Additionally, team members reported hearing a disembodied voice on the stairs that yelled "Hey!" This voice was captured on a camera situated at the bottom of the steps, and on a digital recorder.

The stairway proved rather active for the Shadow-walkers, and they reported a class A EVP at the base of the steps. According to the report: "An electronic voice phenomena caught at the base of the stairs had a male shouting from the beyond, 'Get some help…he needs help.'"

The Luzerne County Ghost Hunters also conducted investigations at the home and reported activity: the sound of a drawer opening in the kitchen, doors opening, light anomalies, and several class A EVPs.

For a time, the home was the bane of local real estate brokers who couldn't sell the property, even at a minimum price. The hauntings and countless stories about the home made it impossible to even think of selling. Some realtors didn't even want to show the property because of its creepy reputation and no one, it seemed, wanted the "cursed haunted house" on their listings.

The Times Leader, fascinated by the weird tales coming from the property on Welles Street, published several stories about the place over the years, reporting on the haunted happenings and even the eventual but sporadic sales of the home.

In 2013 the Welles house, often billed as one of the most haunted houses in the state, was up for sale once again.

The home's last resident and owner, Katherine Watkins, had purchased the property in August 1982. At that time, the four-bedroom home with two-thousand-plus square feet of space had found its way on the foreclosure list. Watkins thought it was a real bargain for the price of $20,000 and she snapped it up. She didn't care about its haunted reputation.

She was perhaps one of the longest lasting residents in the home, remaining there from the time of her purchase in 1982 until her death in 2013. After her passing, Watkin's family put the house on the market and enlisted the help of Katherine's friend and neighbor Betsy Summers. In the past, Summers had run for office in the city, and this, combined with the home's reputation, again attracted the local press. The headline in the *Times Leader* for April 4, 2013, begged the question: "Is House a Scary Good Deal?" The paper noted that property listings for the home stated that it was an "authentic haunted house."

"City resident Betsy Summers, who lives across the street, designed the advertisement hoping to stir up interest in the 46 S. Welles St. property. The owner, Katherine Watkins, died last year, and Summers said she is trying to help the family sell it. Summers said she's not making up the haunted claim, which has been detailed in several published reports. 'It has a pretty nasty reputation,' she said."

Summers had written the listing for the house, trying to hype the home's history in a way that would appeal to those interested in the paranormal, by dubbing it an authentic haunted location. Despite the publicity, there were only a couple of parties interested initially, mainly due to the terrible tales associated with the home. When the paper asked Summers about her personal experiences in the house, she had little to say: "I take care of what I have to do and get out. I try to ignore any noises I hear."

In recent years there have been rumors the Welles house was condemned and scheduled to be torn down, but still it stands. Public records show the home was last sold in 2019.

Over the years, various paranormal teams and ghost hunting shows attempted to gain access to investigate the home, but to no avail.

A previous listing on an online real estate site noted the home's ghostly reputation: "Come to Welles St. for a haunting good time. This 1800s home needs a care keeper for its ghostly inhabitants. 10' high ceilings 1st Fl, 9' high ceilings 2nd Fl. Laundry rm on first Fl can support a ½ bath. Much of the old charm remains with the home. View the pictures and you may see some of the ghostly orbs."

So, the house at 46 South Welles Street now sits abandoned. No one has lived in the home since 2012. The front door and windows are boarded up, a hopeful deterrent against squatters, vandals, and drug users. But such defenses merely serve to keep out the human element.

Although it sits quiet and closed off, many people still quicken their pace when walking past the home. Standing before it, one has the sense that there is something within, waiting patiently for an innocent home buyer, or the next curiosity seeker. No boards or barriers can affect whatever it is that lies inside the building, which by many accounts is something very dark and disturbing.

A Brief History of the Welles House

My Start in the Paranormal
Dave Spinks

I became intrigued by the paranormal in 1986 after an experience I had as a young man. I saw my maternal grandfather standing at the foot of my bed while I was at my dad's house. Normally, that would not have been that big of a deal, except that it was a bit after three AM and my mom's father lived thirty miles away. He would have had no reason to be at the foot of my bed, or even at my dad's house at that time of morning.

As I remember the incident, I woke from a dream, sat straight up in bed, and there he was as plain as day. I rubbed my eyes and looked again. I said out loud, "Papa, what are you doing here?" He didn't respond. He just smiled and looked at me. I did the old double-take and closed my eyes, asking myself if I was really seeing this or if I was dreaming. I opened my eyes again and he was gone, so I chalked it up to a dream.

My papa was a WWII veteran and was a chain smoker of unfiltered cigarettes for many, many years. He had a quarter of one lung left as a result of the smoking. He had an oxygen tube permanently fixed in his throat, and he had to have oxygen constantly to avoid suffocating. He would often smoke a cigarette out of the hole through his throat.

Because of his illness, I was naturally worried about him after the dream, so I called to check on him the next day. I was surprised when my uncle from out of state answered the phone. When I asked him what he was doing there, he responded, "Nobody called you yet?" I said no and I will never forget his response: "Your grandpa died last night." I just dropped the phone down to my side because I knew in my heart that he had come to say goodbye to me before he went wherever he was going.

I didn't tell anyone about the dream I had or my grandfather visiting me until approximately six months later. I was afraid my family would think I was nuts.

We were all at papa and mama's house for dinner, the first time most of us had been together since papa's funeral. We were at the table eating and out of nowhere, I just came out and told everyone what had happened the night papa died.

One by one, all their faces went white, and their eyes opened wide. There was an awkward moment of silence, then suddenly it was like an explosion. They all started saying they'd had the same "dream." Some of them were excited and some were scared shitless about it because we all came to the realization that it wasn't a dream at all, he had come to each of us to say goodbye. From that moment on, I knew there was something else after we die. I began to pursue answers almost immediately after this experience.

My Start in the Paranormal

Disclaimer
Dave Spinks

The following events that you will read in my investigation journal are my personal recollection of what transpired during my time inside the haunted Welles house in Wilkes-Barre, Pennsylvania.

I must emphasize that what you are about to read is based on my personal experience and perception of the events that transpired. Evil locations can affect feelings, thoughts, even the physical body. I experienced all of this and more while investigating the Welles house and the events continue to have repercussions on my life today.

Other investigators, even those present at the same time I was there, may have different recall, understanding, or feelings about what occurred. This does not, in any way, invalidate anyone's experience. Actually, it strengthens the case because it shows just how much dark entities can interfere with humans.

I have retained all facts to the best of my own knowledge while telling my personal story. Some identities have been changed, or are composites, in order to both protect and respect the privacy of the individuals involved.

This is the story of what I experienced and the changes it caused in my life.

The Investigative Journal of Dave Spinks
Dave Spinks

The Beginning

I felt a rush of adrenaline as I prepared my equipment for the six-hour trek to Pennsylvania from my home in West Virginia. My destination was a house located at 46 South Welles Street, a house with a notorious reputation.

I'd been given some information on the home in the weeks prior to my departure. I was a bit apprehensive as I took a short break from packing my gear and I thought about what I had learned regarding the different families that had lived in the house. Most of them had not stayed in the home very long. Stories circulated around the community about the families that had lived there. At first, they appeared to be normal, average people, but after living in the house on Welles Street, many of them got divorces, became alcoholics, heavy smokers, and had financial problems. Additionally, there were several deaths associated with the house. Three were suicides. Two of those were hangings, and the third, the most disturbing, was a teenage boy who died of a self-inflicted shotgun blast. There was also a report of a man who dropped dead from a heart attack on the front porch of the home.

There were other, reportedly accidental, deaths, too. A man was said to have been crushed by his horse against a tree in what is now the backyard of the house. The tree is still there.

Thinking about the coming investigation, I couldn't help but wonder if the land was cursed or if the trouble was all inside the home.

Was something inside, some presence, causing such terrible things to happen to the people who chose to live there?

I continued packing up my gear, checking off each item as I packed it away in cases and duffel bags. As I was doing all of this, my wife was telling me how unhappy she was, both with the pending investigation, and the fact I would be away for so long. I explained to her that this was a once in a lifetime investigation and there was no way I would miss it.

This statement would prove far truer than I care to admit.

Day 1

My gear was loaded, and my truck was filled with gas. I headed over to a friend's hunting camp to pick up some firewood for the wood burning stove in the house on Welles Street. It was October and the nights in Northern Pennsylvania could get into the low 30s. After loading up half a truck bed of firewood, I turned on my GPS and started my trip from Southern West Virginia to Wilkes-Barre, PA. I was about two hours into my trip, listening to Metallica, and filling up on Coca-Cola, my preferred form of caffeine, when my phone rang. It was James Johnson. I answered and could hear James, along with Jerry Howard, talking in the background. They had both arrived at the house late the night before, and they wanted to know when I would get there. They both sounded excited and a bit nervous. I told them I had about four more hours of driving to go. James said, "Dude, you're not going to believe what happened to us last night. Get your ass here now!"

I was a bit startled because of the tone of his voice. Was he nervous, scared, or excited? It was difficult to tell. I had investigated with James numerous times, and I had never known him to get rattled. He is very solid in his beliefs and a pretty religious guy. He started explaining to me that when they arrived at the house, they carried their gear in and decided to do a walk-through and check it out. He told me as soon as they entered, they felt an overwhelming heaviness. As they walked from room to room, they kept hearing thumps and bangs all over the house. He said they continued down into the basement and it got even creepier. James told me as they climbed down the stairs into the basement, just off to their right they heard a loud hiss. He said the hiss was so loud they were convinced there was some kind of animal like a snake or cat down there with them. They looked around for a few minutes, then quickly went back upstairs.

As I was listening to the story, I could feel the hair on my arms and the back of my neck stand up, and I was getting ice-cold goose bumps all over my body. From that very moment I was sure there was something malevolent in the house on Welles Street.

Four hours later my GPS said I was a mile away. I could feel excitement and tension building as I followed the directions. I was sitting at a stoplight about a block away, cussing and telling the light to hurry up and change. I was both nervous and anxious to see the house and get started. Finally, after what seemed like an hour, the light turned green. I made a left turn, drove about a quarter of a mile, and there it was, the sign for South Welles Street. I stared at the street sign as the GPS called out in a British woman's accent to turn left. I made the quick turn on the one-way street and began looking for the house number while watching the GPS to see how far away I was.

As I made my way up the street, I noticed all the houses were right on top of each other, with only a few feet of space separating them. Suddenly, the GPS announced I had arrived at my destination, but it was wrong. The GPS was off by two houses for some odd reason. Ignoring the GPS, I looked at the numbers on the homes and found the correct house.

I parked on the curb in front of the building and sat there for a moment. I couldn't take my eyes off the place. It was dark now, but still the house had an overwhelming, creepy aura about it. It seemed like it was pulling at me. I almost felt like I was in some kind of trance and moving on autopilot.

I mounted the steps up the porch and the front door sprang open. Jerry, James, and a third man, Sam, were all there to greet me. They all said it was about time I got there.

The first thing I noticed was the expression on James's face. I had never known him to get shook up or anything major while on an investigation. But now he had a sort of deer-in-the-headlights look about him. I asked him if he was okay and he replied, "Dude, this place is fucked up!"

All three of them started talking at once about the hiss and how much it had freaked them out. James said after the walk-through they decided to bed down for the night. I asked if they were all in separate rooms. "Nope, we all sleep down here in the living room close together."

At the time I thought this was pretty hilarious. Three grown men so wigged out that they all slept on the living room floor on their air mattresses. I gave them some ribbing about it, and they told me to just wait, and I would see for myself. Little did I know what was in store.

Not wanting my manhood to be compromised in any way, I said "I'm not scared; I'll sleep in one of the rooms by myself."

They all laughed and replied, "Yeah, that's what we said."

Jerry and Sam went to the kitchen to get some drinks while James began to tell me more about the events of the previous night. He said after the hissing incident they broke out some gear and went back into the basement to do a quick session to try to get some responses. They felt that something was pissed off because they were in the house. James said while using a hack-shack ghost box, they were hearing demonic sounding growls and references to the devil.

While he was telling me this, I kept hearing bangs and knocks from the upper level. James's eyes were as big as ping pong balls, and he knew I was hearing the same thing he was. We knew no one else was in the house, and the other two guys were within sight in the kitchen.

James continued to tell me about how they were all bugged out and decided to put a stop to the ghost box session and turn in for the night. He also described how he'd hardly slept at all because he kept feeling as if someone were staring at him. He described it as an overwhelming feeling of someone standing right in front of him, looking at him dead in the face, yet no one was there. At one point in his sleepless night, he saw a shadowy figure in the doorway of the kitchen and dining room looking at them while they were trying to sleep. All the while during his telling there were continued thumps and bangs coming from upstairs. I resisted the urge to just run up and check it out, my attention divided between James' telling and the unknown noises.

James finished his tale and Jerry and Sam came back into the living room, suggesting we all unload the gear from my truck. "Are you guys hearing that thumping and banging coming from upstairs?" I asked. They said it had been like that since they arrived. I thought it may be caused by the property's old water pipes and plumbing but I was doubtful. I knew we'd need to try and debunk the sounds because they were so loud, they would interfere with our audio recordings.

In the course of unloading my gear, I ended up alone with Jerry for a few minutes. He said, "Dave, there's something I have to tell you about James." I asked what was up and he went on to tell me about the previous night. "Last night, when we were sleeping, I woke up and James was standing by the front door with all his bags packed. He was ready to leave." I thought Jerry was kidding me and I said so, but he shook his head. "No man, I'm not joking. I saw him standing there, it was like he was in a daze. He was holding his crucifix in one hand and rubbing it between his fingers. I asked him what he was doing, and he said, "I gotta get out of here man, this place is not good! It's not good at all!"

I asked Jerry what he did about the situation. He told me it took him an hour to calm James down, but when he finally did, James lay down and went to sleep.

I was blown away by this because, as I previously stated, I had worked with James on several cases before, and in spite of some pretty hairy investigations, I had never seen him so much as flinch. We finished unloading and went back inside the house. The guys asked if I was ready to see the place and I said, "Hell yeah!" I couldn't wait.

We started from the foyer at the base of the stairs and went up a huge staircase to the second floor. At the top of the stairs was a small bathroom with a shower-tub combo, a toilet, and a small sink. It was the only bathroom in the house, and it was absolutely filthy.

A landing at the top of the stairs led to the bedrooms. One very small room to the far left, then another bigger room, then another room right next to the bathroom. That room had an adjoining room you could get to by walking through it. This was in the oldest part of the house. That bedroom had a back staircase that went down into the kitchen.

I was surprised to find that all the rooms still had some furniture and odds and ends from the last owner who had died almost two years prior. I asked Jerry about all the stuff and why it was still there. He told me the family kept having estate sales trying to get rid of as much as they could before they hauled everything else to the dump. The house was full of dust and cobwebs and had a musty odor. Obviously, a cat had stayed in the small bedroom upstairs because it stunk to high heaven of cat urine. Most of the walls in the house were also stained yellow from years of cigarette smoke from previous owners.

We proceeded downstairs back into the living room. There were two couches, two end tables and a wood burning stove. A huge doorway led into the dining room containing a nice, large dining table with eight chairs and a hutch. Beyond that was the kitchen.

So far, I had felt some heaviness while on the stairs and in all the rooms upstairs—particularly the small room and the first big bedroom—but the kitchen conveyed a truly weird feeling. I noticed right away that it was fully furnished as if someone were still living in the house. There was a kitchen table, dishes, utensils—the whole nine yards. I felt uncomfortable seeing all the stuff there knowing the owner of the items was deceased. The sensation was somber and somewhat disconcerting.

As we were walking through each room, Jerry pointed out where it was believed people had committed suicide. The room upstairs that reeked of cat urine was supposedly where a teenage boy had shot himself, the living room was the spot where a man had hanged himself. To the back of the kitchen on the right was the staircase that led up to the back bedroom. This was the oldest part of the home and was once quarters for workers of the large plantation that once defined the property. At the back of the kitchen was another door leading to the basement. We proceeded down the steps to the spot where, the night before, all the action had taken place.

As I walked down the stairs, I could smell the dampness. The original blocks were intact, made of hand-cut stone, and you could see where water had leaked in and filled the basement during past heavy rains. It was rather large, dark, and creepy. As I walked from the front to the back, I noticed a small stool and an ashtray full of cigarette butts sitting in the middle of the floor facing the front of the house. We would later learn from a neighbor that she would often find the previous owner of the home sitting in the pitch dark, smoking cigarettes and having a conversation with someone or something unseen. I found this information rather unnerving. As I got to the end of the basement toward the front of the house, I noticed a separate, small room with a coal chute. This space was formerly used to store the family's coal to keep warm during the harsh Northern Pennsylvania winters.

As I was standing there, we started hearing thumps and bangs coming from above us on the ground level. We decided to go up and see what was going on. James and I crept quietly over to the bottom of the stairway and listened intently. We were transfixed by the continued knocking and banging coming from upstairs, and we attempted to pinpoint exactly where the sound was coming from. Everything in me told me the noises had to be from the water pipes, but as my brain was trying to rationalize the sounds, they would suddenly change location, direction, and pitch. Each time we thought we had it figured out, they would be somewhere else, and no rational explanation was making sense. Additionally, we knew the furnace had not been turned on, so nothing logical was adding up. Jerry and Sam came over and joined the discussion, but they couldn't make sense of the sounds either.

We decided to go upstairs and spread out around the house so we could find an explanation for the noises. When we reached the top of the stairs, we all went to different rooms. As soon as we did, the sounds stopped. It was as if something intelligent was taunting us. We walked around each room in bewilderment at what had just taken place. All we could do was shake our heads in disbelief.

We moved back downstairs and decided to get our game plan together. As we were talking about our plans for the investigation, the noises started back up again and this time they were louder. We ran upstairs hoping to catch whatever was causing the sounds, but for a second time, the racket stopped as soon as we reached the rooms. Now I was convinced something was really screwing with us. We went back downstairs, a bit more on edge, and went back to planning for the upcoming investigation. Since it was getting late, with a lot of investigative work to do the next day, we decided to turn in for the night.

The guys all laid out their air mattresses on the living room and dining room floors. I chuckled to myself again at the behavior of these grown men and decided I would sleep in one of the rooms upstairs. I took my air mattress up to the second floor and went into the second room on the left. I set up my sleeping area and lay down for the night. At first everything was fine, and I began to fall asleep. Out of nowhere, a loud banging started like someone was hitting heavy metal pipes with a monkey wrench, and it was coming from the room I was in. I sprang up off my mattress and ran to the top of the stairs. I shouted down to the other guys and asked them if they were trying to screw around with me. James replied in an aggravated voice and asked what I was talking about. Apparently, my shouting had woken him up. I called down and asked if they had heard the loud banging noise and I couldn't believe it when they replied they'd heard nothing. I asked again, finding it ridiculous they hadn't heard the sound, and this time they all chimed in that they'd heard nothing. I was slightly pissed off at this and headed back to my air bed to get some sleep. I was mumbling to myself and thinking if they tried it again, I would sneak down and catch them in the act.

I climbed back into bed, totally exhausted from the drive, and just wanting to get some rest. I must have been asleep for about an hour or two when I was awakened by a super cold breeze on my face. It was so cold it actually made me shiver. I chalked it up to the house being old and probably not insulated very well. I covered my face with my sleeping bag and tried to fall back asleep. Suddenly, the banging started again. I tried to ignore it for a minute or two, thinking once again it was the guys trying to screw with me. Without getting up I yelled for them to knock it off. There was no response from any of them. I yelled once again, this time louder. "Guys, knock it off, for real!" Again, there was no response. I was getting more pissed off by the second.

Just then, I felt what can only be described as someone or something sitting down on the edge of my air mattress. Every hair on my body stood up and I realized the room was now freezing cold. So cold that I could see my breath. It took a second for my body to react to what was happening. I jumped off the mattress and hauled ass downstairs, skipping every step I could without breaking my neck. When I got down to the living room, I was really expecting the guys to be sitting around laughing at me because they had scared the shit out of me. To my surprise they were all sound asleep and snoring away. I sat on the couch for a few minutes trying to gather myself. I decided right then and there that I would be sleeping on the couch in the same room as the rest of the team for the duration of the investigation. I arranged my pillow and sleeping bag on the couch, hunkered down, and tried to calm my nerves. Lying in my sleeping bag trying to get comfortable, I tried to ignore the ever-present noises going on throughout the house. I couldn't help but sense we were being watched by numerous sets of eyes from the kitchen and foyer areas. I finally covered my head with my pillow and went to sleep.

The next morning, when we got up, the guys saw I was on the couch and I got the old "We told you so didn't we?" I proceeded to tell them what had happened in the bedroom and they all swore they had nothing to do with any of it. I believed them. After that, the second room upstairs was dubbed the hell room.

Once I got some caffeine and a shower, I decided to go back into the hell room and take some readings. I used a Mel Meter to see if there were any significant EMFs (Electromagnetic Fields) in the room. To my surprise nothing over a 3.0 was recorded. I did, however, notice a large black candle in the corner of the room on a small table. I thought this was strange because you don't usually see black candles unless they are being used in some kind of ritual. I took some readings around the candle and again, there was nothing above a 3.0, so I paid it no more mind. I went back downstairs and reported my findings to the rest of the team. They were all ready to go out and get some food before the night's investigation, so we headed out.

Driving away, my mind remained on the house. I was still bothered by all the items left by the former, deceased owner. Were some of her prized possessions among the objects in the home? Was she still attached to them, or was the activity in the home caused by something else? Hopefully, our investigation would reveal some answers.

Day 2

We spent the day working on setup for our investigation of the Welles house. There were cables to run, DVR cameras to set up, and equipment checks to verify that everything was in working order. We were doing a livestream of the investigation online so there was plenty to do.

James and I did a walk-through of the house with a Mel Meter and Sam followed us with a camera. As we documented the EMF readings, I would call out the numbers for the camera so that everything was documented. We noticed the readings were unusually high around the staircase. About three quarters of the way up the stairs, I got a huge spike on the Mel Meter. We were in the middle of the stairway and there was at least a twenty-foot ceiling. The meter read 6.6 mG (milligauss), well beyond a normal reading.

Little did we know at this point, this spot would prove to be one of the most active areas in the house. Our findings would lend credibility to the story of one of the prior resident's daughters. The young woman apparently tripped at the top of the staircase, but instead of falling down the steps, she felt as if she were grabbed by something and carried safely to the bottom of the stairs.

We continued our walkthrough, documenting the EMF levels in all the rooms on the upper level of the house. There were no other significant readings beyond the 6.6 mG spike on the stairs. On our way back down the steps, we again noted a climb in EMF at the midway point, and we also noticed a cold spot in the same area. I decided to do a quick EVP (Electronic Voice Phenomena) session right where the cold spot was.

I took out a digital voice recorder and asked three questions in succession, then played the recording back. There were no responses, so we decided to see if the spirit, or spirits, could manipulate the Mel Meter on command. We started with a steady reading of 2.7 mG and asked the spirits to make the meter go higher. Right on command, the Mel Meter began to climb. First to 3.0, then to 3.1, then 3.2. Sam started provoking a bit by saying "don't be a wimp." As soon as he said that the meter went to the 3.5 mark we had asked for. We asked for those numbers to be held and they were, then the numbers started to climb again, continuing to 4.0, then 4.2; the numbers went all the way to 4.9. It was as if something wanted to show us how powerful it was. It seemed that whatever we were dealing with was intelligent.

After a few more moments on the stairs, we decided to go down to the basement and check the readings from the electrical box. Just as we suspected, the electrical box and the uninsulated wiring in the basement were putting off a huge amount of EMF in the immediate area around them, but there wasn't much bleed-over. The lack of bleed-over made it clear that the box was not the cause of the unusually high readings around the stairs and the air above them. We noticed the EMF readings around the stairway would fluctuate wildly, so we decided the spot warranted further investigation. I grabbed a camera and James started talking to the spirits, asking them to come back to the stairs and communicate with us. He placed a single flashlight on the middle of the steps and asked the spirits to grab it, kick it, throw it, whatever they could do to demonstrate to us that something intelligent was there. As he was saying this, the flashlight came on all by itself. This sparked our curiosity, so we continued to ask questions. James asked it to turn the flashlight off. When it didn't turn off immediately, James said, "You can't take six years to do it, we need immediate responses from you in order to show us it is really you manipulating the flashlight."

Before he even finished his statement, the flashlight turned off.

This prompted him to further verify something was manipulating the light, so he asked again for the spirit to turn on the flashlight. Again, nothing happened. After about ten seconds, he said, "I'm going to count to five, and when I reach five, turn the flashlight on. 1…2…3…4…5…" Again, there was nothing, so we decided to switch gears and try another EVP session on the steps. James started by asking the spirits to talk into the black box with the red light.

On playback, we heard the name "Bishop." James asked about Bishop but there was no response. While he was asking questions, I kept seeing strange light anomalies on the camera screen. They were unlike the dust orbs I had seen on many investigations prior to this one. I hadn't seen any bugs in the house either, but up to this point, I just kept watching the screen and listening as James asked questions and listened for responses in playback on the digital recorder. James made several more attempts trying to get EVP responses, but there was still nothing. Again, while he was playing back the recorder, I saw some amazing light anomalies on the camera's view finder, but I said nothing at the time.

James shifted gears and began to provoke more. He told the spirits that we would be playing some Jewish prayers in the house, and that we had a Dybbuk box we were going to open. (A Dybbuk box is an item said to be haunted by a restless or malicious spirit. The name is of Hebrew origin.) James continued to taunt and challenge to get a response on the recorder. After three or four minutes of this, there was still nothing, so we decided to move to the next phase of the investigation.

James reached for his flashlight and discovered it was dead even though fresh batteries from a new package were put in it thirty minutes before we started. Battery drain is something paranormal investigators experience often. It can happen to freshly recharged batteries, or brand-new batteries straight out of an unopened package. One of the theories associated with this is that spirits will drain the batteries in order to gain energy to try to manifest or communicate. In my years investigating the paranormal, I have seen this kind of battery drain occur many, many times.

James continued with his line of questioning. He asked the spirits if we should be afraid a Dybbuk box was in the house. As he was asking this, I continued to witness multiple light anomalies both on and off the camera screen. These were all recorded, and we observed them later during playback of the DVR cameras. The light anomalies were blowing my mind, but I continued to bite my tongue so as not to disrupt the EVP session. I was hoping we would catch EVPs that coincided with the light manifestations. At one point, James asked "Are there any spirits here that need help?" In response we heard a "clink-clink" sound, as if two bottles were clanking together. James and I both said "kitchen" at the same time. We were assuming the other two guys were in the kitchen making noise, and we wanted to annotate the recording, so we would know it wasn't an EVP. Just then, Sam came up and asked why we had both said kitchen. We told him we had heard what sounded like bottles clanking and assumed they were in the kitchen getting drinks. Sam assured us he had not been in the kitchen. He went back to the control center to double check with Jerry, then came back and confirmed with us that Jerry had not been in the kitchen either. We couldn't believe it because the sound had been so loud and clear and we were sure they were the cause. Furthermore, we had caught the sound on our recordings, too, so we had it both on tape as well as having heard it with our own ears. As an investigator, this is some of the best kind of evidence, so we were quite excited about the incident.

We decided to try another EVP session and ask the spirits if they could recreate the sound we had heard. James also asked if the noise was related to the Dybbuk box, and if they could tell us what the noise was. This time on playback we had a very clear response: "Don't care." It was a class A EVP, and again, it was outstanding evidence since it was a direct response to what we were asking. We played it back numerous times, and everyone agreed the clear response was "Don't care." No other responses were recorded during those three questions, but when any kind of response is captured, it's best to keep running with it until all the activity stops, so we went right into another EVP session. Furthermore, the strange light anomalies were continuing and were being captured on the DVR camera placed directly in front of the stairs.

Sam began to go over some of the information about the last woman who had lived in the house when Jerry yelled out "Oh shit!"

We all responded, rushing over to the control area to see what was wrong. Jerry told us the basement door had started to move, opening on its own then slamming shut, then opening and closing again. I still had the camera rolling and I aimed it at the basement door, filming it as it began to open of its own accord. The door stopped moving and we set about trying to debunk the incident. There was an exterior door right next to the basement door, and we checked for any kind of breeze coming in that would have blown the door closed. There was no wind at all, and even if a random gust had come in, it would not have explained the door opening by itself. This was amazing to us since it demonstrated that something had manifested to physically manipulate the heavy door, causing it to open and close right before our eyes.

As we got closer to the door, we started to use various meters at the basement entrance to check the readings. I still had the camera rolling and we were taunting the spirits to slam the door again, but nothing further occurred. Jerry shouted out again, and both he and Sam got very excited because they both saw a shadow figure peek out from the basement and look at us.

We placed a static meter at the entrance to the basement. The instrument was designed to detect static electricity in a 360-degree radius. The principle is based on the belief that when spirits manifest, there is a strong, static electricity charge in the area around the manifestation.

Some people can feel static electricity with their own bodies while doing investigations. Most often it's noticeable by the hair on one's arms and neck standing up. The static meter is a great visual tool since it lights up in various colors when there's activity. It will also indicate the direction the energy is coming from. As James placed the meter at the top of the steps, Jerry and Sam went to control to check on our live feed. I moved to the top of the stairs and started to ask questions.

"Who's down there? Show yourself." No sooner had the words left my mouth when the static meter lit up like a Christmas tree, not once, but twice. I could also feel the static charge on my face and arms. The house felt alive with activity, and the longer we went, the stronger it was getting. Jerry and Sam headed down to the basement to conduct a spirit box session to try to make contact with whatever seemed to be hiding down there. As James and I were helping them set up for the session, I started having problems breathing. At first, I thought it was the musty air in the basement, but then realized it felt different. I felt as if I were in an oxygen-deprived environment, like being at a high altitude, and my breathing became more and more labored the longer I was in the basement. I started to have a slight tickling in my throat, and I began to cough repeatedly. I told the others I was having a hard time breathing and I headed back upstairs. I figured I would monitor the DVR system while they conducted the spirit box session.

Jerry had carried the Dybbuk box down to the basement. He set up a 360-degree static meter, an Ovilus 3, a device that spirits can use to issue words, and a spirit box. The spirit box was a modified AM/FM radio that scans through active radio stations very quickly, thus creating a white noise effect. The theory behind such devices is that entities can utilize the scanning to communicate. Jerry started by asking, "Where are you?" James and I, listening in on the monitors upstairs, both heard the verbal response of "behind you." Simultaneously, the Ovilus said "danger." Jerry continued to ask questions and a woman's voice came through the box saying "demon." Jerry asked several questions pertaining to a possible demon, but there were no relevant responses to his questions on the topic.

A female voice came through clearly and said "who?" Jerry responded by asking who she was. She did not respond, but a male voice came through very clearly and said leave. Jerry responded that he wasn't going to leave until the spirit stated its name and he reported that there was shadow movement all around him in the basement.

James, Sam, and I were all monitoring him on the cameras upstairs when we started hearing loud banging noises coming from upstairs. I decided to go and check out the sounds and told James and Sam to keep an eye on Jerry via the cameras. I grabbed a flashlight and a camera and made my way quietly over to the stairs. I was hoping to capture something on camera. As I got closer to the stairway, I heard what sounded like people having a conversation upstairs in one of the rooms. I couldn't make out what they were saying, but it sounded like there were around four or five people talking. I could still hear the knocking and banging noises, but they were not as loud as previously. I started making my way up the steps. It was pitch black and I was looking through my camera's night vision viewfinder as a guide to make my way up the stairs without tripping. I was moving as slowly as humanly possible, not wanting to disturb whatever was talking upstairs. As I drew closer to the top, the voices became louder and louder, but I still couldn't make out what was being said.

It felt like it took me an hour to make it to the top of the stairs, but I hadn't made any significant noise and the voices were still talking. They were now the loudest they had been since I first heard them, and I believed they were emanating from the far back room on the right. I continued at a snail's pace down the hall to the middle room. Now the voices were even louder, and I knew I was headed in the right direction. There was a wall to my immediate right and I knew as soon as I got past that wall, I would be in visual range of whoever or whatever was talking in the back room.

I eased along the wall very slowly. I moved my camera forward so I could point it around the corner. This way only the camera, and not my body, would be in sight of whoever or whatever was in the room. Little by little I moved in the pitch blackness, edging the camera to the end of the wall. The talking was still very loud, and I struggled to make sense of what the voices were saying. It sounded like babbling whispers, that's the only way I can describe it. The camera was now pointing into the room and coming into focus. It focused first on the doorway and then the room. I couldn't see anything on the view screen. I could still hear the talking but the room appeared to be completely empty. I paused for about fifteen seconds, hoping something would show up on the camera, all while praying the audio was catching the voices I was hearing.

I decided to leave my place of concealment and head ten feet toward the doorway of the backroom. Two feet forward and I could still hear the talking, yet there was still nothing on the camera's viewfinder. I kept moving forward until I was a foot away from the doorway. I took a slow, deep breath. I was going to go into the room fast and hard to see if I could capture the source of the voices on video. I counted to myself, 1...2...3 and I sprang into the room. As I crossed through the doorway the talking suddenly stopped. I scanned the room with the camera, and there was nothing. Nothing at all. I couldn't believe it. I stood there in bewilderment at what had just happened. I kept scanning the room, looking for something, anything, to explain what I had just experienced. I said a few choice words, taunting the spirits to show themselves on the camera. The voices did not return, but something else did happen.

I felt what I can only describe as a cold finger touching my right arm. Every goose bump on my body came to life and I was startled so badly I couldn't move out of the room fast enough. I dashed back downstairs to the control center. I didn't say anything to the other guys, other than I couldn't make out what I had heard upstairs. I went back to monitoring the live feed from the basement where Jerry was still conducting his spirit box session. I couldn't figure out what I had experienced upstairs, and I wanted to just set it aside for the moment.

In the basement, Jerry had started playing a Jewish prayer as a trigger to see if it would provoke any responses. If there was something negative in the house, this might cause it to react. There is a synagogue just a few doors down from the Welles house, so we thought that Jewish prayers may yield something. Jerry asked again for the spirit to identify itself. The spirit box issued some clear responses including the name "Beelzebub" and the phrase "the one." Jerry asked how many souls were trapped in the house. Again, there was a clear response from the box; it said, "Seven." After this, the box spat out several clear phrases including "the fire's inside," and "we're burning." We would later find some factual evidence linked to the home's history to back up these strange comments from the spirit box.

Jerry continued the session, asking if there was a demon holding the spirits of the dead in the home. There was no response. He then asked if there was any way they could be helped in escaping the house. Out of the box came a loud "NO." Jerry then stated that he was getting goosebumps and he asked the box if he was in danger. Immediately we heard an evil-sounding, female laugh echo throughout the basement. It was a mocking laugh, and it was very creepy. Jerry asked several more questions but there were no relevant responses until he asked, "Is there any human spirit here that can tell me the name of the demon that is responsible for holding human souls in this house?" Immediately Jerry heard something in the far-left corner behind him. He was startled for a second and, of course, he couldn't see anything at all in the pitch black of the basement. There was no light except the faint glow coming from the equipment in front of him. He reached out to turn off the spirit box and right as he reached for it, the box said again, "Beelzebub."

He ended the session, and we decided another team member

should go to the basement and continue. James and I decided to go down together. We didn't waste any time. We went downstairs and took up positions with the equipment. We stated that we wanted to talk to whatever had been communicating with Jerry. The Ovilus 3 was running and right away, it said "hurt you."

We knew from our research it was the former owner's birthday, so we wanted to try to communicate with her. We got out a digital recorder and tried an EVP burst session, asking three questions quickly. Checking the playback, we heard a loud response, but it was unclear what was being said. It was clear, however, that something was trying to communicate. We turned the spirit box back on to see what kind of responses we could get. We asked, "Are you out of the Dybbuk box?" The response was, "I can't breathe." We continued to ask more questions and the box kept repeating things like "get out" and "leave." We wanted to ask about the Dybbuk again, so we said, "Is the spirit from the Dybbuk box trying to work with the spirits of this house?" This time there was a clear response of yes. We had some kind of confirmation about the Dybbuk at least. We utilized the spirit box for a few more minutes but there was nothing else relevant.

We then tried to entice the spirits to communicate with us by asking them to touch some of the devices we had set up, like the static meter and a flashlight. We ran a recorder at the same time, hoping to catch some audio evidence. During this I started to get a very bad stomachache. I asked James how he was feeling, and he too said his stomach was bothering him. After about ten minutes of no activity, we broke out a different spirit box, this one the SB-7. It works the same as other ghost boxes, but it's always good to mix things up and try different devices. Once the box was up and running, we asked the spirit to tell us its name. There was an immediate, clear response of "demon." The same word was repeated two more times. What we didn't know then, but would learn later during evidence review, was that at the exact moment the word demon was being said, the live stream camera started freezing up.

We proceeded to ask more questions. We asked if there was anyone buried on the property. A female voice responded "me." We continued to ask questions but received no intelligent responses other than the word demon being repeated over and over. I heard what sounded like a loud hiss, but it didn't come from the spirit box. James turned the box off and asked if I had heard the noise and I confirmed we both heard the same thing. We tried to call out to whatever was making the hissing sound, but we heard nothing else, so returned to the spirit box. Upon asking what had just hissed at us, the quick response was "demon." We also noticed it had become noticeably colder around the Dybbuk box.

There was nothing else coming through the box, but James and I both felt like we were being touched. Something unseen was touching my right hand, and James said he felt something touching his head. We were both still experiencing nausea, but we continued to ask questions. We challenged whatever was touching us to do something more, knock something over, or show itself to us. With no other responses, we ended the session and headed back upstairs to convene with the rest of the team. After a short break, Jerry said he was going to go back down into the basement, and this time he was going to play a Muslim prayer in an effort to get something to respond. About three minutes into the prayer, Jerry said he was being touched by something. Like us, he started to challenge whatever was touching him to do something else. He reported feeling the touch on his left arm and reported seeing a shadow off to his left side in a doorway. He got up and walked toward the shadow, telling it to come over to where he was. He continued to taunt the spirit and tell it to touch the devices. He saw something else move in a corner of the room. He berated the spirit, calling it a coward and telling it to do something more or to communicate.

As he reached over to the spirit box, he pulled off the respirator he was wearing and started to gag as if he were going to throw up. After a moment of this, he stated he was feeling very sick. He turned the recording of the prayer off and started to state how weird it felt in the basement. He started gagging for a second time, and again stated that he felt as if he were going to throw up. Still, he continued with the taunting. "If you don't do something right now, I am going to play this prayer every day that I am here." While he tried to goad the spirits into lashing out and attacking him, the static meter started to go off near him. He started to feel a bit apprehensive about being hurt by something unseen.

He turned on the hack shack and there was an immediate response from it that said, "Stop. Stand down." It was as if something was warning him not to play the prayers anymore. Jerry responded with, "You're going to have to push me. I am not going to stand down!" In an act of defiance, he turned the recorder back on and started playing the Muslim prayer again to further antagonize the spirits. At this, he stated that his back was starting to hurt. He also reported that he felt like his shirt was being pulled on. He asked if there was a spirit touching him and the box responded, "I'm here." Continuing to taunt, Jerry challenged, "Scratch me, punch me." The spirit box replied by stating Jerry's name. Just then, he jumped up and yelled out saying he heard a hiss behind him. Still, he continued with his taunts, asking if that was the best they could do. The ghost box spit out a number of foul responses including "kill, rape," and "kill the devil."

Jerry reported that while all of this was going on, he was hearing weird sounds all around him when the box spat out the name of Jerry's daughter. This really got to him and he went off on the spirit, taunting it harder: "Come on, you don't scare me. I know you're nothing but a bullshitter!" The use of his daughter's name was a bit much, so after a few more moments, Jerry ended the session and came back upstairs.

We took a break and regrouped, talking amongst ourselves about what we would try next. It was decided that James and Sam would go up into the hell room and do a ghost box session and an EVP session. At first, there was nothing significant coming through. Then the name Kay started to come across on the hack shack. This was significant because the name of the home's last owner was Kay. Sam asked if Kay was there with them and the box responded, "I'm here." This was picked up on later in evidence review, but Sam and James did not hear the response then. Not hearing the answer, they decided to sing happy birthday to Kay, and after they finished, the box replied with a quick "thank you." Unfortunately, Sam and James didn't hear this answer either, so no other questions geared towards Kay were pursued. They tried some EVP sessions, but there were no responses.

While the guys were upstairs, I was with Jerry, trying to help him out. He was still feeling sick and still felt like he was going to throw up. About forty minutes had passed since his extreme taunting of the spirits in the basement. When James and Sam finally came down from their session in the hell room, I was still trying to help Jerry. He reported that he felt like something had punched him in the face and eyes, and they did indeed look physically swollen. I attempted to help him clear himself of whatever had attacked him. I sprayed holy water on him, and he immediately started to feel better.

These types of physical effects were something that we all dealt with during our time investigating the Welles house. It was a sign of just how powerful the forces in the home were.

James was visibly shaken by the situation and he started to read St. Michael's prayer in hopes of ridding the house of whatever negative energy was still affecting Jerry.

We made a collective decision to stop all investigation for the night, since things were obviously becoming dangerous.

Day 3

We decided to take a break and go get some food before we started the next night's investigation. As we left the house I felt as if a huge weight lifted off of me. The further away from the house we got, the lighter I felt. I asked the other guys if they felt like this and they all said yes, they noticed the same thing. This was very consistent during the course of our investigation of the Welles house. As soon as you got in the place, there was a very heavy and oppressive feeling. It felt as if something was breathing down your neck the entire time you were in the house and it never let up. But upon leaving, there was an immediate experience of feeling lighter.

Once we got back, we decided to start the night's investigation upstairs in the oldest part of the house. This section had been servants quarters for the old plantation. At one time there had also been a fire in this section of the house. James and I tried an EVP burst session. I asked the spirits to make a loud bang or knock to let us know they were there. On playback, clear as a bell, we heard a response: "Get out." I continued with questions based on the response, asking who it was that told us to get out and asking for a name. I also asked, "Are you in this room or another room of the house?" Again, there was a response, this time saying, "I'm not."

We decided to keep going with the EVP session and asked, "Are you the one that has been attacking us in this house?" Just then, James reported smelling something bad. I couldn't smell anything since my nose was plugged due to sinus problems. I continued with questions, asking "Are you one of the people who committed suicide in this house?" James chimed in with "Get out? Was that a warning or a threat?" We then heard a loud boom that was clearly upstairs with us but we knew the other two investigators were outside having a smoke break. I fired off more questions and the whole time, I could feel the hair on my arm and the back of my neck standing at attention. There were no further responses on the recorder. We tried another burst session and still nothing, so we concluded that whatever had answered twice had either left or moved to another area of the house. That, or it simply didn't want to, or couldn't, respond to us anymore.

We moved out to the main staircase where we had been getting huge EMF spikes and set up to conduct a ghost box session using the SB-7. Right away, the box started saying "murder" and "help." We asked who needed help and "me" came through the box. We continued by asking for a name and trying to find out how this person had died. A male voice from the box started giving us more responses. "Bishop" came through; we had heard this before in the house. We asked the spirit if he had killed himself and the response was "men." When we asked how many men there were, the response was "two."

As quickly as it had started, the line of response from "Bishop" came to an end. There was nothing else from him, or related to, his death. We changed tracks and asked, "Who else is here on the stairs with us?" We started hearing a woman's voice come through the box, but there was nothing related to our questions, so we asked if there was anyone else that wanted to communicate with us. We received a clear yes response and asked who was speaking. There was no response.

James asked, "What is the easiest way for you to communicate with us." The response from the box was "chalk." James asked the spirit if it wanted us to bring it chalk; the response was "scribble." He continued by asking why it wanted a chalk board and the voice responded, "you'll see."

I started asking again for one of the spirits to tell us their name. This time, the box responded "Dave." I was taken aback by this since the box was now saying my name, and I doubted there was a spirit there by that name, so I asked, "Why did you say Dave?" The response sent shivers down my spine because the box said, very clearly, "Spinks."

I realized the significance of this spirit, or entity, whatever it was, knowing my first and last name. We were communicating with something that was definitely intelligent. Once again, the communication switched gears and we started to get the name, or title of Bishop again. We tried to get more information related to this person, but the responses were vague in nature. This would not be the last time Bishop would come up in communications.

We ended the session and went back downstairs to regroup and determine the next phase of our investigation. We were all beginning to feel as if our energy was being sucked from us at a very intense rate. As soon as we came downstairs, Jerry said he wanted me to go down to the basement. He was insistent I go right at that moment, but I told him I needed to regroup. He wasn't aware something upstairs had stated my first and last name, but I needed to process it myself.

We had a DVR system set up in the house with six different cameras placed in various rooms around the home. On the feed from the cameras, we were seeing all kinds of light anomalies and camera distortions. The motion detector on the basement camera lit up numerous square boxes at once, indicating movement of some sort. Strange shadow play was going on in a couple of the rooms. There was no one else in the house, but it was as if the place had come to life.

James and I were watching the activity right in front of our eyes and our jaws were wide open. We couldn't believe the number of anomalies and looked at each other in disbelief. There were literally hundreds of them happening simultaneously in multiple rooms of the house. It was both amazing and frightening to witness.

Jerry asked James to go down to the basement by himself and conduct a session to see if he could communicate with the dark entity that we believed was down there. I was still a bit shaken by the earlier communication upstairs and something stating my name, so I opted to monitor the camera feed while James did his session. Once in the basement, he attempted to turn on a spirit box. The power was dead, so he put in fresh batteries and attempted it again. Still nothing. The spirit box simply wouldn't work. Battery drain isn't the only thing common during paranormal investigations. Equipment failure is also commonplace, and this seemed to be what was happening. James took out yet another set of new batteries and tried the spirit box for a third time. This time it came on and he asked who was with him. "Beezel," came the reply. We knew the name was short for a known demonic name. While we heard the response on the live camera feed, James didn't catch it. We told him over the com what came out of the box. He was a bit unnerved, but he asked the spirit again for its name. Again, the same response of Beezel came through. The box continued to state the same name, and it was apparent to me that James was growing more and more concerned. I could see the worry on his face as he asked if Beezel was the one that had been bothering us. The spirit box replied with a loud yes. The box continued to say Beezel on its own repeatedly, then suddenly said "Ouija."

This was very creepy. It was as if something was telling us to use a Ouija board to talk to Beezel. James continued with his questions, asking what had happened in the house. There was a clear response of "murder." There were noises all around him at this point, and he nervously looked over his shoulder into the pitch blackness of the basement. He turned on his flashlight for a quick look behind him but saw nothing.

Watching James, I could tell he was becoming more and more uncomfortable. He started to fidget around, then stood up and looked around nervously. His next question was, "How many of you are down here with me right now?" The box responded quickly with two distinct voices saying "many." Now he was even more nervous and started looking from side to side and behind himself. He asked if the spirits wanted us to leave or stay and there was a response of "stay." He asked the question a second time for clarification and received the same answer again.

At that moment, the box turned itself off. There was no explanation as to why it did this. James reached over and turned the box back on, asking the spirits if they were connected to the house or the land. This time the clear answer from the box was "native." I considered this important since the whole area was once a thriving, sacred area for Native Americans.

James asked if the response meant native to the land. The box quickly responded yes and then shut itself off again. Again, the brand-new batteries were completely drained. Normally, new batteries would last for hours and not just minutes. Once James had the box back up and running, he asked who kept messing around with the box. Again, the reply was the name Beezel.

James was even more bothered at this point. He turned the spirit box off and picked up a digital recorder. Right away he found these batteries also drained, even though fresh batteries were in place at the start of the session. He put the recorder aside and turned the spirit box back on. Before he even asked a question, a voice from the box said, "I'm gonna getcha." James was done. He switched the box off, looked around the basement for a few seconds and then headed back upstairs. When he came up to control, we asked if he was okay. He said he couldn't breathe down in the basement. It was clear to us something negative was affecting him in many different ways. We were concerned about him and kept asking if he was all right. Jerry and Sam took him outside to get some fresh air. Just as they closed the door, I heard what I can only describe as the most insane screeching sound coming from down in the basement. It was so loud that it hurt my ears. It also scared the shit out of me. I jumped up and ran out of the door to ask the other guys if they had heard the sound. None of them had heard anything. I knew something was letting me know it was pissed that it didn't get to finish what it was attempting to do to James.

Jerry and Sam decided to go back to the basement and play the Muslim prayers again in an attempt to bring forth the negative entity. They wanted to piss if off. I was against this since it wasn't how I do things, and with James already being affected so negatively, I didn't think it was a good idea to push the envelope just to capture more evidence.

Jerry and Sam went ahead and moved forward with their plan. They mixed it up some by playing both Muslim and Jewish prayers. After about five minutes of this, they turned the recordings off and turned on a spirit box, hoping to get responses from the negative entity in the basement. The first thing out of the box was a voice telling them to get out. It was evident that something wasn't happy about the prayers having been played. Jerry said they weren't leaving, and again a voice came over the box telling them to get out. Once again, Jerry stated they were not going to leave. At that, the spirit box shut itself off. At the same time, Sam looked at the EMF detector and saw there was a 4.0 mG reading. Jerry kept trying to get the spirit box to turn back on without any luck. Something in the house apparently had enough power to affect electronic equipment.

We decided to wrap the investigation up for the night and Jerry and Sam came back upstairs. We were all physically and mentally exhausted, but the events of the night were not over. Sam looked at Jerry and asked him if he was all right. He replied "no." As we were all gathered around, Jerry began to become very agitated. James and I stepped outside to get some fresh air, leaving Sam and Jerry alone in the house. After a minute or two, Sam came outside and joined us. After talking a bit, we all went back inside. Jerry was working on a piece of equipment and James said he still wasn't feeling well from his experience in the basement. Sam started looking around because he had misplaced his crucifix. He realized he'd given it to Jerry and asked him if he still had it. Jerry said no, he'd given it back.

This bothered Sam. He didn't have his crucifix and he didn't remember Jerry giving it back to him, so he continued to look for it. After a few minutes, he came back and asked Jerry again if he was sure he had given it back. Jerry insisted he had, and Sam said it was okay and they shouldn't argue about it. Jerry said, "Something is manipulating your mind here, man." Sam replied with "Whatever, man. You're the one that has been saying, 'where is this' and 'where is that' all day today." The whole thing escalated into a huge, screaming argument with each of them accusing the other of various things.

James and I tried our best to defuse the argument and calm them both down, assuring them this wasn't a big deal and they needed to settle down, but the argument continued to become louder and more aggressive with each of them going back and forth. Finally, they decided to go upstairs and continue the argument away from the two of us.

James and I sat down in the living room, hoping the guys could work it out with each other. They continued to scream at one another, and it could be heard all throughout the house. It must have lasted for about forty minutes, and I just knew this evil house was trying to divide and conquer us one at a time. They finally separated from each other, and everyone started to do their own thing, arranging gear, and checking equipment. I was growing increasingly concerned about James. He didn't look quite right and was acting a lot different than normal, becoming very withdrawn. I decided I would have a talk with him after all the gear was put up for the night. I looked for him in the living room, the last place I'd seen him, but he wasn't there. He wasn't in the kitchen either and as I looked throughout the house, I realized he wasn't anywhere inside. I checked out back and on the front porch, but he was still nowhere to be found. Finally, I assumed maybe he was in the bathroom and I sat down to check my social media feeds while waiting for him to come out.

A while later, Jerry came running from the control center yelling and screaming that James had left. I replied, "What do you mean he left? You mean he went to the store, right?" Jerry was freaking out and said, no, James had left and wasn't coming back. Right away, I grabbed my phone and started dialing his number. There was no answer. I must have called him a dozen times and I became super worried about him. Jerry and I both continued to call but neither of us made contact with him. We didn't know if he was alive, dead, possessed, or what. It was turning into a worst-case scenario and I knew that it was all because of the damn house.

We kept trying to make contact with him, sending him messages on social media, text messages, and continuing to call, but still nothing. After about an hour, Jerry grabbed a camera and said he wanted to film and talk about the effects of the house. I was against it, but Jerry was insistent that it needed to be documented, so we started filming. Jerry was seriously pissed off at James for leaving. Sam and I were more worried about him than irritated since we didn't know if he was okay.

It seemed to me that the only thing Jerry could focus on was the house and the investigation. For me, it was another sign that something in the house was trying to manipulate us and I was disturbed by what it was doing to us all.

We continued to try to contact James, and after about three hours of not knowing what was going on, he finally called back, in tears. He apologized for leaving but said, "I can't be in that house for another second, Dave." I told him not to worry about it and asked him where he was, but he wouldn't tell me. I kept telling him I was worried about him and just wanted to be sure he was okay. Jerry refused to even talk to him. James finally told me that he was in a hotel about ten miles away and he needed to get some rest. He said he was exhausted from constantly being messed with in the house. I told him I understood and asked him if he needed money or anything else. He said he was fine. I told him to get some rest, have a good breakfast in the morning and think things over, then let us know what he wanted to do. He said okay and hung up.

Jerry had been on the front porch chain-smoking cigarettes and cussing James for leaving the investigation. He heard me get off the phone with him and came back in, asking if James was coming back. I told him James was exhausted and needed some rest so he wouldn't be back that night. Jerry went into a cussing fit, saying James taking off was bullshit. He went on and on and it took Sam and me over an hour to finally calm him down. Again, it was another indication of whatever was in the house exerting an influence on us all. Exhausted, we finally called it a night.

I didn't sleep well at all. I had a dream about a dark, shadow figure that was leaning over James as he slept. Its face was just inches from him, and it was doing something with its hands over his head. It was laughing the most evil, demonic laugh you could imagine, and talking in a language that sounded like Latin to me. It would talk a bit, then laugh, talk a bit more, then laugh again. It was almost as if it was doing some kind of incantation or something. In the dream, all I could do was stand there and watch. I couldn't move, I couldn't speak. I tried to yell out to James, but nothing came out. I tried to yell out for him to wake up, but again, nothing came out. Finally, I started saying a prayer in my head. "Saint Michael, the Archangel, defend us in battle." Before I could get the next word out, that thing snapped its head around and looked right through me. It let out a very loud snarl, stood up, and started to come at me. I was frozen. I couldn't move an inch, couldn't scream for help. It got right in my face, so close I could smell and feel its putrid, hot breath. It reached its arm way back like it was going to strike me, and I suddenly woke up in a cold sweat. My heart was pounding like it was going to come out of my chest. I shook myself fully awake and realized what an insane dream I'd been having. Or was it really only a dream? It felt as real as anything I had ever experienced in my life.

Day 4

It was seven in the evening and we were getting ready for the night's investigation. We still had no word from James about whether or not he was going to return. We put fresh batteries in all the equipment, checked that everything was working properly and began to set up. About thirty minutes before our start time, James came through the front door. I was really relieved and told him it was damn good to see him and asked if he was okay.

He said he was all right and that he was ready to investigate. He told us he had prayed all night and cleansed himself of an evil entity trying to attach itself to him. He explained how while he was doing his cleansing and prayers, he heard a loud, bellowing howl as the entity left his hotel room. He also explained that we were all in true danger, but he also knew we were not going to quit the investigation, so he wanted to be there to support us in case we were attacked as he had been. I told him Jerry was really pissed off, and he should go hash things out with him away from us. He agreed and went into the kitchen to find Jerry. They talked for a minute, then went outside on the back porch to speak in private. They came back in about twenty minutes later, laughing and joking with one another, so I assumed they had worked out any differences they had. We were now ready to take on the house and whatever was in it once more.

As we were about to start, I got a call from my wife. She was hysterical and started telling me how she'd had vivid dreams that she was being attacked by demons all night long. She said she wanted me to quit the investigation and come back home. I calmed her down and told her she was just worrying about me. We were already having problems in our relationship, and the whole time she was talking I was chalking it up to her not wanting me to be anywhere without her. This marked the beginning of the end of our relationship.

I was not going to quit the investigation. I'd never heard of a team living in, and investigating a known, haunted location for such an extended amount of time and I refused to let this opportunity slip away. After I got off the call, I went back into the house and prepared myself for the night's investigation. Jerry came over and asked me if I would use a Ouija board that night. I chuckled at this, because he had already asked me, and I had made it clear to him that I would have no part in using a Ouija board. He pushed the issue and asked me why I wouldn't use one. Again, I explained to him that I didn't use the boards, and to please not ask me again. He finally said okay and walked away, but this topic would continue to be a source of tension between us for the rest of our time at the Welles house.

He then approached James and asked if he would use the Ouija board that night. To my surprise, James agreed. After everything he had experienced the night before, I couldn't believe James would use one. I pulled him outside away from Jerry and Sam and tried to have a serious talk with him about the Ouija. "Look man, I know you don't use them, why have you all of a sudden changed your mind?" I asked. James replied, "Oh man, they aren't bad. Everyone uses them, they're just another tool to try and communicate with spirits." I reminded him that when you use a Ouija board, a spirit or entity uses your body to manipulate the planchette. He told me he didn't care and that he was going to try it anyway. I spent about twenty minutes trying to convince him it was dangerous, but he wouldn't budge on the topic, so I gave up. After all, he was a grown man free to make his own choices. I couldn't help but wonder if he had really gotten rid of the negative entity he said was trying to attach to him, or if he was, even now, being controlled by it.

We went back inside, and I made it clear to the rest of the team that I was opposed to them using the Ouija board, especially after everything that had happened in the house. I also told them I would be there to back them up if it all went crazy. After all, we were there to document any and all paranormal activity by using different means to communicate.

Let me explain a bit about my misgivings regarding Ouija boards. I do not myself condone their use. In my personal experience, a large portion of negative hauntings that I have investigated have a connection to the use of a Ouija board. I'm referring to residential cases where the people experiencing the activity have, at some point prior to the haunting, used a Ouija board in the home. These cases have included people being scratched, choked, suffocated, held down, and even burned. To me, there is no such thing as coincidence, and having investigated hundreds of residential hauntings with the boards involved, well, you do the math.

Jerry and James set up in the middle room upstairs for the night's session. They took out an old Ouija board and various ghost boxes. We wired the room up with every piece of paranormal equipment known to man. I was given the job of writing down the letters spelled out by the Ouija board when questions were asked. Sam had the camera rolling, and Jerry and James sat down at the table with the board. Jerry donned headphones with white noise playing in order to take away his hearing. He also taped half of a ping pong ball to each of his eyes to take away his sense of sight. Additionally, he put on a respirator to restrict his breathing.

In a sense, he was doing a version of the Ganzfeld experiment at the same time he was using the Ouija board. Typically, the Ganzfeld experiment was used to test a person's psychic and telepathic abilities. I thought this was even more dangerous since he was allowing himself to be more open to the spirits in the house by using sensory deprivation techniques.

Once everything was set up, James started the session by "opening" the Ouija and telling the spirits in the house to come and communicate through the board. He announced that once the board was closed, they would have to leave and could no longer communicate through it.

Jerry started with the first question, asking if there was a demon in the house. After about a minute, the planchette started to go in circles on the board. Jerry asked again if there was a demon in the house. To my amazement, the planchette went to "yes" and stopped. Jame's eyes got really big. Jerry then asked what the demon's name was. The planchette went back to the center of the board for a moment, then started going in circles. It went to the number five and stopped. James and I glanced at each other. We were puzzled and didn't yet understand the significance of the number five. James then asked, "Do you mean there are five demons in this house?"

The planchette circled around the center of the board again before moving to the word no. At that moment, the audible alarm on the Mel Meter went off. It was sitting on the table right next to the Ouija board, and the display signaled a .5 degree drop in temperature around the device. If anything, the temperature should have gone up with two people sitting in close proximity to the meter, but there's a theory in the paranormal that if a spirit or entity is trying to manifest, it will affect the temperature in the immediate area.

As I was watching the meter, the temperature dropped seven degrees, going from 68.7 down to 61.7 in an instant. The intensity in the room was now elevated because we knew we were experiencing something significant. Jerry asked the spirit if it wanted to hurt one of us. The planchette responded by going to yes. James's eyes were as big as saucers, and he was visibly shaking. Jerry continued with his line of questioning, asking the spirit who it wanted to hurt. The planchette circled three times and then started spelling. James called out the letters as I wrote them down on the pad. J...E...R...R...Y...clearly the board was signaling out Jerry as the focus of the negative entity's intended attack. Suddenly, as the spelling was completed, Jerry jumped up and screamed, knocking everything off the table, throwing the headphones off and shouting that his back was burning.

I almost fell out of my seat. James was freaking out, saying, "What the fuck is going on? What happened?" Jerry kept saying, "it burns, it burns!"

We scrambled around to regain our composure. The Rem pod across the room started going off, a good fifteen feet away from us. We immediately tried to tend to Jerry's back as he was still crying out that it burned and hurt. I lifted the back of his shirt and there were three giant scratches going from the base of his neck down to his lower back. They were so deep that blood was beginning to ooze from the scratches. I was freaking out and James was out of his mind scared. He kept saying that we had to get out of there right then and there, saying, "Screw this shit man, screw this shit!"

I got out holy water and started dousing Jerry with it. Sam was still manning the camera, trying to catch all the chaos on film, but he too was scared senseless, yelling, and screaming, "Holy shit, holy shit!"

We got Jerry out of the room and back downstairs away from the situation in the room. All the while, I could still hear the Rem pod screaming at maximum volume and the Mel Meter still going off. I yelled at everyone to get outside. We practically ran over each other trying to get out, like a stampede of bulls all trying to get through a door at the same time. Once outside, I continued pouring holy water on Jerry and James started reading St. Michael's prayer. Sam was over by himself, saying prayers.

After about thirty minutes of pandemonium, we started to calm down, and Jerry finally started to describe what he had seen right before his back started burning. On the verge of tears, he told us that he saw a vision of a grayish-skinned figure with horns and cloven feet in the corner of the living room. In front of the figure, there was an old phonograph, and it was playing music from the 1920s. Just music, no lyrics. The figure was holding his sharp, pointed fingernails on the record in order for it to be played and the entity said, "Your soul is mine."

Jerry said there was a rancid smell of death all around this figure and he could taste the nasty odor in his mouth. The thing also had burning eyes.

The horned figure started to reach for him. In his vision, Jerry turned to run, and that's when he felt the burning on his back, which caused him to snap out of the vision and in turn led to all hell breaking out in the room. We decided to go back into the house and review the video footage. To our amazement there was nothing recorded on the main camera. We were dumbfounded.

We ended the investigation for the night so we could further regain our composure after the harrowing events. I couldn't help but sit and look over my notes. The number five kept coming back to me. I kept asking myself, what's the connection? What does the number five have to do with demons? I opened my laptop and did a quick internet search, cross referencing the number five and demons. The second I opened the page, it hit me like a ton of bricks because I saw a quote from the Bible, Mark, Chapter 5:

"And they came over unto the other side of the sea, into the country of the Gadarenes. And when he was come out of the ship, immediately there met him out of the tombs a man with unclean spirit, who had his dwelling among the tombs; and no man could bind him, no, not with chains: because that he had been often bound with fetters and chains, and the chains had been plucked asunder by him, and the fetters broken in pieces: neither could any man tame him. And always, night and day, he was in the mountains, and in the tombs, crying, and cutting himself with stones. But when he saw Jesus afar off, he ran and worshipped him, and cried with a loud voice, and said, what have I to do with thee, Jesus, thou Son of the most high God? I adjure thee God, that thou torment me not. For he said unto him, Come out of the man, thou unclean spirit. And he asked him, what is thy name? And he answered, saying, my name is Legion: for we are many. And he besought him much that he would not send them away out of the country. Now there was there nigh unto the mountains a great herd of swine feeding. And all the devils besought him, saying, send us into the swine, that we may enter into them. And forthwith Jesus gave them leave and the unclean spirits went out and entered into the swine: and the herd ran violently down a steep place into the sea, (there were about two thousand) and were choked in the sea." (Mark 5: 1-13, KJV)

Reading the passage, things began to make sense to me. The entity was letting us know, without revealing its name, what it was. I relayed the information to the other guys. Like me, they were all a bit freaked out, but it made sense to them. It was now clear that things were becoming dangerous. All of us had been affected in one way or another both physically and mentally. James and I had been physically sick; Jerry, Sam and I had all been touched by something unseen; and there were mental effects from all the activity. Jerry wanted to push on and fight whatever had scratched him so violently upstairs. I had said from the beginning that all the provoking could be dangerous, and it now seemed clear that I had been correct, but Jerry wasn't fazed by this in the least. In fact, I think all the activity was making him more obsessed with the whole thing. He shouted out loud to the whole house, "This is my house you son of a bitch and you don't scare me."

He was shouting, cussing, and throwing things around. I noticed his face was kind of distorted, his eyes looked dark, and his voice sounded different. It just didn't look like him. I realized then that Jerry most likely had an attachment. Whether he had gotten it from the Welles house or from some other location, I would never know.

If there was something attached to Jerry, were the rest of us also at risk? James had already dealt with something that caused him to leave the house once and I was having terrible dreams.

Jerry went outside to smoke a cigarette, so I decided to test my theory about the possible attachment. I went out with a bottle of holy water. I came up behind him and asked if he was all right. I was still concerned. He said, "No, I'm pissed that that fucker scratched me." I told him to calm down and that I'd put some holy water on him. He told me not to, that he'd be fine. "No Jerry, you're not," I said, "You just had a huge meltdown in there, man." He again insisted he was fine, and I again said, "NO, you're not," then threw holy water on his neck and back.

He came unglued. He turned around like he was going to punch me in the face. I stepped back and continued throwing holy water on him. This time, it hit his face and it stopped him in his tracks. He seemed to snap back to himself. He was dazed, confused and out of sorts. He looked at me for a moment and said, "Wow, man, what happened?" "You weren't yourself man. I think we need to rethink this investigation; it's getting pretty freaking crazy and dangerous."

Jerry went back to saying he was fine and refused to discuss the matter any further. It was 3:40 AM, and I was calling it a night. I headed back in and found Sam and James spreading kosher salt all around our sleeping area for protection from anything evil. We all looked at each other, agreed it had been one hell of a night, and climbed into our sleeping bags.

But again, I wouldn't sleep well.

I awoke in a panic, covered in sweat from another disturbing dream. In it, a dark shadow figure was hovering over me and I couldn't breathe. It was suffocating the life out of me as I lay there on the couch. I fought with everything I had in me and I still couldn't move a muscle. I tried to yell out for help, and nothing came out of my mouth. I was about to lose consciousness and I was getting tunnel vision. I started saying a prayer, asking God to help me. Suddenly, I came to and sat straight up on the couch gasping for air. I looked around the room, but everyone else was fast asleep. I was breathing so hard and heavy; it was as if I had just sprinted a mile. I wiped the sweat from my head and looked at my watch. It was 4:50 AM.

I suddenly knew that it had not been a dream. I had just been attacked by something evil while I was sleeping. I got up to get a drink of water and James woke up. He came in and asked if I was all right. "Yeah, I'm good man," I said. I didn't want to scare him after all that had happened already. I got a drink of water, then I slammed back a small glass of holy water, hoping it would protect me from another attack in my sleep. I walked back to the sleeping area and sprayed holy water all around us. James asked what I was doing, and I told him I felt like putting down some extra protection.

Needless to say, I didn't get much sleep the rest of the night.

Day 5

I woke up feeling like I had been beaten with a baseball bat. My whole body ached, and I was extremely tired. In fact, the whole team was extremely beat. It's an exhaustion that's hard to explain. Like coming down with the flu, feeling totally fatigued, with deep aches and a feeling as nasty as you can imagine.

Jerry had to fly back home for the weekend, and Sam had to go back to his day job. James was going to take them both to the airport that evening. We went out to get a bite to eat, then stopped by the local library to do some more research on the house. We were hoping to uncover more information on the history of the place and about what had gone on there.

Going through public records, we soon learned the rumors we had heard from some of the area's longtime residents were true. Time after time, the house was bought and sold, repeatedly, year after year. A family would buy the home and not long after it would be sold in a tax sale. Often, this was only within a couple of months of the previous sale.

We spent hours researching, and it was finally time for Jerry and Sam to head to the airport, so we headed back to the house to retrieve their luggage. I was the first one up the steps and as I put the key in the lock, I heard footsteps running up the stairs just inside the front door. My years of law enforcement training kicked in. I immediately suspected someone had watched us leave the house and had broken in to steal some of our equipment. This wasn't too surprising, as the house wasn't in a very good neighborhood. I pulled out my firearm, turned the lock, and flung the door open. I immediately ran inside yelling, "Stop you son of a bitch, or I will shoot your ass."

I went up the stairs and started clearing each room as I was trained to do. All the while, the other guys were yelling and asking what the hell was going on. I told them to stay where they were and to watch the sides of the house for anyone that might come running out. The first room was clear, so was the second, then the third, and finally, the last room upstairs. There was nothing.

I went back downstairs and cleared the ground level of the house room by room. Again, there was nothing. Finally, I went down to the creepy-ass basement. I was sure I would find the intruder hiding in the darkness. After flinging open the basement door and turning the light on, I yelled down, "Ok you son of a bitch, I'm giving you ten seconds to come out with your hands up, or I'm coming down there and you're not going to like it if I have to come and find your ass."

There was no response, so I bent down with my .45 leading the way. I wanted the first thing the bastard saw to be the business end staring him in the face. As I leaned my head down to get a good view on my front sights, I saw nothing. I crept down, taking one step at a time slowly, all the while concentrating on my front sight. As I cleared the entire area downstairs, I couldn't believe it. There was no one in the damn house.

How could this be? I stood there scratching my head because I knew I had heard heavy footsteps running up the staircase as if someone was trying to get away. I made my way back to the front door where the guys had positioned themselves so they could see both sides of the house. They were pretty worked up and yelling at me that they had seen nothing. They all wanted to know what was going on and why I'd gone into commando mode.

I asked if any of them had heard the footsteps running up the stairs inside, and they all said no, they hadn't heard anything. They were looking at me like I was flipping nuts. I asked them again if they were sure that they hadn't heard the running. They all shook their heads and James asked if I was okay. "Yeah, I'm fine," I said. "I know what I heard; it was loud heavy footsteps running up the stairs as I was opening the door."

They just kept looking at each other and I was getting pissed off. I yelled into the house, talking to it like it was a criminal, "okay, you like to play games, don't you? Okay you bastard, you got me this time, it won't happen again."

Little did I know what was in store for me later that evening.

The guys were a bit hesitant about going into the house to get their gear. They knew I was a no-nonsense guy and that I wouldn't fool around about these kinds of things. I never pull my weapon just for shits and giggles, and they knew it. We filed into the house and went about our business. Jerry and Sam started gathering their gear for their flights, and James took out his cell phone to look at his social media.

I went to the kitchen, grabbed a soft drink, and then sat down by myself on the couch. I was still trying to make sense of what happened. I replayed the scenario over and over again in my head, and finally, after a bit, I chalked it up to its being an entity of some kind in the house.

It was starting to get dark, and Jerry and Sam had their gear by the door. Jerry said he was leaving all the audio up and running while he was gone, but no video. I thought this was odd at the time. James asked if I was going to be okay by myself in the house while he was gone. I told him I'd be fine and that if anything crazy happened, I'd just go wait in my truck until he returned. I had no clue then that the next seven hours would be the longest of my life.

Jerry, James, and Sam walked out the door. They all looked back at me with the sort of look that said "poor bastard" all over their faces.

I knew what they were thinking without them saying a word. I knew, because it was the look I'd had in many situations during my time in the military and law enforcement. It was the look you gave someone who had landed an unlucky assignment that was highly dangerous. While no one wanted the job, someone had to suck it up and get it done. In this case, my job was mainly to guard the house and all our equipment from any riffraff that may be lurking around, watching the house, and waiting for an opportunity to steal something.

After the guys walked out, I shut the door behind them and locked myself in. I then realized I was a complete dumbass to be in the house by myself after all the crazy things we had experienced. I shook it off, grabbed my computer and sat down on the couch. I figured it was a good time to distract myself with social media and chat with some of the folks that had been watching our live broadcast from the house.

The feed was still on so people could hear the audio from the stationary cameras. Immediately people started typing messages in the feed's chat room. Someone told me that I had balls of steel to stay in such a crazy location alone. I chuckled and told them that there really wasn't much choice since someone had to watch things. We had about $30K worth of cameras and other paranormal equipment in the house.

People in the chatroom rambled on and on, saying there was no way they would do it. Then one of them suggested that I do a ghost box session. I immediately declined. I didn't want to stir anything else up while I was alone in the house, but people kept on, goading and pleading that I do something. Finally, I relented and told them I would do an Ovilus session. The chat room blew up with excitement. I grabbed the Ovilus 3, sat down in front of my laptop, and typed into the chat that I was starting.

As soon as I turned the device on it spit out the word "devil." I immediately got cold chills from head to toe. People were reacting with excitement; they had all heard the word via the live feed. I couldn't read the comments fast enough, so I focused on the device instead. I asked, "Is the devil in this house?" The Ovilus responded with the name Mark. I continued, asking if its name was Mark and who Mark was. There were a few more seconds of silence, then another word issued from the device. "Five."

Shudders went through my whole body. I knew right then and there it was talking about the passage from the Bible, Mark Chapter 5, that referred to demons being taken out of a possessed man by Jesus, entering swine, and the swine then leaping into the ocean.

I started shaking. I grabbed the Ovilus to turn it off. I'd had enough already. There was no coincidence the device was letting me know there was something evil there. I thought to myself, screw this man, I'm done. I typed in the chat room to let people know I was done with the session. They all started begging me to continue, like a bunch of addicts needing another fix.

As I was explaining to them that it wasn't safe, out of nowhere, I heard what sounded like twenty people upstairs talking amongst themselves. Just like the previous occasion, I couldn't make out exactly what they were saying, but it was loud. I asked the people in chat if they could hear it over the audio feed. Some people heard it, others couldn't. I started to describe to everyone what I was hearing; all the while, the sound was getting louder and louder.

Finally, I grabbed my sidearm and ran upstairs to see if anyone was in the house. Again, I went through the process of clearing each room, and again, there was nothing. No living people, no voices, nothing. I sat back down at the computer, my senses in overdrive as I continued to chat with the people online. Then, all hell broke loose.

I heard what I can only describe as something as big as an elephant running up and down the stairs. It was so loud it felt like the house was shaking with every massive step. I jumped up yelling, "What the fuck is that?" I scanned the foyer looking for the cause of the sound. I ran out, sidearm in hand, to the stairway, and as I reached the steps the noise suddenly stopped. I was relieved for a split second, then it felt as if the house came alive.

The talking started again. It sounded as if someone was on the outside of the house, running from window to window and pounding on each one. The pounding was so hard, I expected the windows to shatter at any second. I followed the sound with my eyes, first at the dining room window near where I was, then to the front porch window, then around to the side of the house, and finally to the back.

I realized no one could possibly cover that much ground that fast, so I ran out the front door in order to meet whoever was doing it head on. I figured it had to be a group of kids or something. They probably knew we were there doing a paranormal investigation and wanted to have a little fun and try to scare us. I sprinted around the side of the house. There was no one there. I continued all the way around the house and found nothing. I just could not wrap my mind around the fact that this was not a living person doing these things.

I came to the realization that whatever was in the house was powerful enough to manipulate things in a way unheard of. The front door was still standing wide open. I walked back in but made up my mind that I would not spend another minute alone in such a hell house. I grabbed my phone and immediately left. As I got in my truck, I felt defeated and unnerved at what had just happened. Right away I started receiving messages on my social media asking if I was okay.

I didn't want to deal with anyone at that point, so I just ignored the messages. I was simply overwhelmed. Thirty minutes later I had regained some of my composure. I answered some of the messages of concern that had come in. People listening to the feed had heard the thunderous footsteps and the banging on the windows. I told people I was fine and would be sitting in my truck since I needed some space to process what had just happened.

In truth, I was going to leave. I started the truck and put it in gear, but something stopped me. To this day, I don't know why I stayed. It was as if the house had some kind of hold on me. I sat there with the truck running for what seemed like an eternity. The last thing I remembered was looking at my watch. It was 4:00AM.

Day 6

I woke up at the break of dawn. I was still sitting in my truck with the engine running. It was about 6:00AM. My mind was still foggy, and I felt like I'd been in a car wreck. I was sore, and my bones ached. I drank down half a bottle of soda, took some aspirin, and tried to pull myself together. After waking up some, I called James to see how far out he was from his airport run. His phone rang and rang but there was no answer. I waited about five minutes and redialed. I was relieved when he finally answered, and I asked him how far away he was.

"I'm at a gas station about two miles from the house," he said. I was ecstatic with the news and told him he wouldn't believe what had happened to me the previous night. James then told me he'd been at the gas station for hours, debating on whether or not he was going to even come back to the house.

"What? You're freaking kidding me, right?" I sputtered. I couldn't believe what I was hearing. I told him what had happened while he was gone. He said he already knew since he had been getting tons of messages from people in the live feed telling him I was in danger and the house had gone crazy.

"I'm not going to lie to you man," he said. "I'm scared to death of that house and I feel like something very bad is trying to attach itself to me." I reminded him that his clothes and gear were still at the house, and that it was very dangerous for me to continue to be alone in the place. "I don't want to get any of my stuff out of that house," he said. "If it's been in that house, it's tainted. I don't want any of it. If we're both smart, we should call it a day and just leave and never go back."

I knew then I was going to have to do some serious talking; otherwise, James was going to leave the investigation and head home, leaving me to fend for myself alone in the evil Welles house for two more days. I also knew in my heart that he was right. We talked back and forth for about half an hour. Finally, I told him to stay there, that I was coming to meet him, and we would go grab some breakfast and talk.

I headed down to the gas station. When I arrived, I pulled up next to his car on the passenger side and I saw him sitting there with his phone in one hand and his crucifix in the other. His eyes were closed, and I knew he was praying. He hung up after about five minutes and I got out of my truck and tapped on his window to let him know I was there. He came unglued, his whole body flinching madly in fright. I chuckled a little as he rolled down the window, cussing at me and saying, "You scared the shit out of me."

We found a place to eat, grabbed a table, and ordered food and drinks. I looked at James and said, "How about this, we'll stay out of the house today and tonight and we'll go hang out at the mall. Then we'll go out tonight and do something fun." James looked at me for a minute, then said, "Dave, you don't understand. Man, I was talking to my priest when you pulled up. He agrees that something is really trying to hurt me in that house. I really don't know if I can risk going back in it at all. Ever!"

He proceeded to tell me the only reason he was even considering staying was that Jerry had promised to pay him for coming. Additionally, he didn't want to leave me by myself in such a demonic location. As James was talking, I noticed how much better I felt. The heaviness was gone, and I felt as light as a feather. My mind, body, and spirit were clearer, just being away from the Welles house. I was in a great mood. I started joking around with James, trying to lift his spirits as well.

By the time we finished eating, we were both in much better spirits, but James was still far from deciding on whether or not to go back into the Welles house. We spent the day at the local mall in order to stay away from the home as long as possible. After several hours, I suggested we go down to the local church and get a bunch of holy water to take back with us. I said, "Let's get enough to really soak it down." James's eyes lit up and he agreed.

When we got to the church, I grabbed two spray bottles out of my truck. I intended to get them filled. James looked at me and the bottles and shook his head. "Oh, my God, they are going to think we are crazy," he said.

I told him all we could do was try and see what they said. Once inside the rectory, we were greeted by a couple of nuns. The nun working at the window asked how she could help us, and I said, "Yes, ma'am, we need some holy water." Before I could say another word, she said okay and disappeared. Obviously, she hadn't seen the large spray bottles I was holding. She came back with a small, standard bottle of holy water used in the church. I politely thanked her and said, "We sort of need more than that."

I lifted the spray bottles up so she could see them. Her eyes got rather large but without missing a beat, she explained she would need to take those to the priest since they didn't have that much ready. She grabbed the bottles and disappeared for a second time. James had his head down as if he was embarrassed. After about ten minutes, the nun returned with two full, freshly blessed spray bottles full of holy water. She looked at us and said, "I hope you boys will be okay."

"Yes, ma'am, we're just doing some major cleaning," I said. She made the sign of the cross and said, "God be with you," and we left. I felt very empowered, and I could tell that James did, too.

We went back to the gas station and retrieved his car, then talked about our plan for the night. There would be no investigating. We would simply go into each room, say St. Michael's prayer and spray the entire room down with the holy water.

I felt relieved. I knew this would be my last night in the house before I went home to spend a couple of days with my son. When we got back to the Welles house, we were on a mission and we meant business. Once on the front porch, James started praying:

"St. Michael, the Archangel! Glorious Prince, chief and champion of the heavenly hosts; guardian of the souls of men; conqueror of the rebel angels! How beautiful art thou, in thy heaven-made armor. We love thee, dear Prince of Heaven! We, thy happy clients, yearn to enjoy thy special protection. Obtain for us from God a share of thy sturdy courage; pray that we may have a strong and tender love for our redeemer and, in every danger or temptation, be invincible against the enemy of our souls. O' standard-bearer of our salvation! Be with us in our last moments and when our souls quit this earthly exile, carry them safely to the judgment seat of Christ, and may our Lord and master bid thee bear us speedily to the kingdom of eternal bliss. Teach us ever to repeat the sublime cry: Who is like unto God? Amen."

While he was praying, I was spraying him, myself, the front porch, and the front door with the holy water. When we finished, we went into the house and repeated the process, one room at a time, top to bottom, until we ended up in the basement. We had expected some reaction from the house, but there were only a few odd sounds which we chalked up to the normal moans and groans of an old house. Things changed when we reached the basement.

James was saying the prayer as I sprayed holy water everywhere. When we reached the middle of the basement, all hell broke loose again. There was an extremely loud growl, followed by a loud hissing sound and a cold blast of air that went right by us. I almost jumped out of my boots; James began to shake. He stopped saying the prayer and froze up. I yelled at him to keep going, to keep praying as I continued spraying all around us with the holy water and spraying our bodies with it as well.

James snapped back to awareness and continued the prayer, this time with more feeling and more faith. I joined him as we finished walking through the basement; then we went back upstairs. We were both very relieved and empowered by what we had done. The house was a lot different. It felt almost light and airy. We decided to watch some football and try to take it easy for the rest of the evening. At about eight o'clock, we were getting ready to watch another game when my phone rang. It was my wife, once again in a panic. She told me she had gotten home from work and lay down to take a nap. Once again, she had a dream that she was being attacked by demons. She was yelling and screaming at me over the phone, telling me it was my fault for doing an investigation at a demonic location. She told me I had to leave right then and head back home.

I stepped outside away from James. I tried to calm her down, but she was really nasty and insistent that I come home right then. I kept telling her I couldn't leave James by himself and that our gear was there with no one else to watch it. She started cursing and screaming at me again. It was too much, and I hung up on her. She called me back right away and I told her that if she was that scared, she needed to go to her mom's house and stay there until I returned. She said fine and hung up the phone.

James knew I was having some issues and asked if everything was okay. I just told him my wife was being pissy and not to worry about it. We sat back and watched some more football. The house remained quiet the rest of the night.

Day 7

My alarm went off at nine in the morning. I was excited to get up and get on the road. I'm a night person and always have been, so nine in the morning was early to get up for me. The truth is, I couldn't wait to get away from the house for a couple of days. I hadn't seen my son in seven days, and I was anxious to get home to spend some time with him.

Jerry called in with his flight information and we put him on speaker phone. He told us Sam wasn't coming back because of his work schedule. Jerry and I thought there may be other reasons why Sam wasn't returning but we left the matter alone. We also learned a new person would be joining us for the rest of the investigation, a woman who was a tarot card reader and went by the name Bambi. When James and I heard the news, we rolled our eyes, figuring that Jerry had another agenda behind inviting a girl named Bambi on an investigation.

I asked James if he was going to be all right. He'd be alone for a few hours in the house before he left for the airport. He said he'd be fine and had already decided to sit in his car and watch the house from there.

I fueled up the truck, hit the interstate and set the cruise control. I cranked up the radio, feeling how great it was to be away from the house. I wanted to put it out of my mind as much as possible. When I reached home, I went straight over to pick up my son. He was at the door with his bag, ready to go. I gave him a big hug and we headed to my place. Once home, we ate, played some video games together, and I tucked him into bed, telling him how much I loved him.

I was hesitant to go back downstairs because I knew there was a heated conversation coming. Right away, my wife told me we needed to talk. She proceeded to tell me that, whether I believed her or not, she was being attacked by something evil the whole time I was at the Welles house. She told me that if I went back, our relationship would be over. I thought this was ridiculous. I told her she was angry because she knew there was going to be a woman joining us for the investigation. I knew she didn't want me around other women or away from her. She would never admit it, but it was the truth of the matter because she was the jealous type.

We argued back and forth, but neither of us would budge on the matter. I finally told her that we could talk more the following day, I was tired and needed sleep. I headed upstairs and fell into bed, even though it was only nine in the evening.

Day 8

I woke up to the sound of my son telling me it was 10:00AM. I opened my eyes and realized that I was in the exact same position I had lay down in. I hadn't moved the entire night. I was surprised to realize I'd slept twelve hours, and I knew the Welles house was taking a toll on me. But I felt refreshed and ready to spend the day with my boy. I went downstairs and made us breakfast, asking him what he wanted to do for the day. He asked about a new video game that had come out and I told him we'd go look for it.

While we were out, we decided to see a movie and I rang my wife to see if she wanted to join us. She said no. I knew something else was going on, but my son and I went to dinner, caught a movie, and enjoyed the evening. When we got back home, my wife was nowhere around so I called her. No answer. I texted her and she finally called me back to let me know she was staying at her mom's house. End of conversation.

I knew she had to go to work the next morning and her mother lived an hour away. I blew it off as best as I could, tucked my son into bed and sat down to watch some shows on television. It was nine o'clock, and I was trying to relax, but I kept having this nagging feeling to go to the live video feed and see how the guys were doing at the Welles house. I had told myself that I wouldn't watch any of it while I was on my short break, but I couldn't seem to let it go. The house has a way of calling you to it and I was realizing it more and more. I opened the page and started watching.

Right away I noticed they were in the basement, and I saw all kinds of strange light anomalies on the live feed from the various DVR cameras that were all through the house. I also noticed they were using a Ouija board, and I couldn't help but say to myself, what the hell are they doing? I watched for a bit, then decided to go back to my shows, but I left the live feed up on my computer with the sound down low. This way, I could glance over every once in a while, to see what was happening.

About twenty minutes later, I heard Jerry say, "What the hell?" I looked over in time to see him and James jump up from their seats, the table and the Ouija board falling to the floor. They were looking behind themselves, each asking the other if they had heard the noise and each affirming that they had. They described a growl followed by a hiss and James was telling Jerry it was the same thing that happened when he and I were in the basement.

Shivers went down my spine because I knew exactly what he was talking about, and I could hear it replaying in my mind. The chat room was going crazy, and many people had heard the sounds over the live feed. I turned the volume up more to see if I could hear anything myself. There was a thunderous boom coming from the floor above the guys. They both reacted at the same moment. They ran upstairs to investigate the noise, forgetting the live camera. They could be heard in the distance yelling and moving about.

I started calling and texting their cell phones but couldn't get a response. I figured they had the ringers off for the investigation, but I was hoping they would check their phones periodically. James called me back, hysterical, and said Jerry had a huge scratch mark on his back. He told me he started using holy water and a St. Michael's prayer over Jerry, and when the holy water hit him, he became verbally abusive, yelling, "Don't spray that shit on me!"

When James hit him with the water a second time, Jerry started kicking and throwing stuff around the living room, then flew out of the front door without a jacket. He was out walking down the street in fifteen-degree weather! I told James to go after him and to not give in as something was likely affecting him. James took off after Jerry and I tried to calm down the people watching the live feed by filling them in on chat. I told them the guys were out checking the outside of the house, looking for anyone trying to mess around with them.

James had me on speaker phone so I could hear his progress as he caught up with Jerry. He was calling after him to come back, and after a moment, he caught up with him. Jerry was mumbling incoherently, and James was yelling at him to snap out of it. I told James to spray him again with the water, and as soon as he did it, I could hear Jerry yell, "What the fuck just happened? Why am I out here with no damn jacket?"

I could tell he was really confused. James told him what had just happened to him, and I could hear Jerry's disbelief at the incident. I told James to let me talk to him and he handed Jerry the phone. I asked him if he was okay. "I don't know, everything is kind of fuzzy. I remember being in the basement and then we ran upstairs, and my back felt like it was on fire and that's all I remember."

I told him he needed to trust James, say some prayers, and let himself be doused with holy water until he could snap the rest of the way out of it. He agreed and gave the phone back to James. He took the phone off speaker so Jerry wouldn't hear us, and I told him to spray the heck out of Jerry with the water and make him repeat the prayers before they went back into the house. I told him to call me back when it appeared Jerry was back to normal and we hung up. I knew then that I had to get back to the Welles house as soon as possible.

James called back about twenty minutes later to tell me Jerry seemed okay. He said they had stood outside and smoked some cigarettes while freezing their asses off. I told him they could go back in, but I strongly advised against doing any further investigation that night. James was in favor of that but getting Jerry to agree would be a different story. Jerry seemed obsessed with challenging and contacting the entities and spirits in the house, prodding them and daring them to do something, and pushing the limits to a point that was beyond dangerous, in my opinion.

We hung up, and I thought about the house and how many of the people who had lived in it were said to have self-destructed, and how many of those families were torn apart. James called back a half hour later. He was in a panic because Jerry was all pissed off that something had attacked him. He was going through the house yelling and cussing at the spirits, daring them to do it again in a complete rage. I told James to scream at Jerry that he was leaving, hoping it would snap him to attention. Jerry stopped yelling and asked James what he was saying. "If you don't knock it off, I will leave your ass here by yourself."

I also reminded James that the live feed was still running down in the basement, and that they might want to take care of all the people who were still watching and listening for the past hour. This seemed to help Jerry snap out of his rage. "Oh, shit, I totally forgot about the live feed." They rushed down to the basement and explained all that had transpired to the listeners. I was relieved when he told everyone they were shutting down the investigation for the night. After everything that had happened, it was too dangerous for them to continue. James was still pretty shaken up. I tried to calm him down and I reminded him that I would be returning to the house late the next night. I told him to watch out for Jerry and to not hesitate to call me if they needed anything.

Day 9

I woke up feeling rested, but in the back of my mind I knew I would soon be back in the evil Welles house. I felt both excitement and despair and wondered what kind of insane experience was waiting for me. I spent the rest of the day with my son, walking around the lake and taking in the sights, trying to relax while the pending trip played out in my mind. Around three o'clock, I dropped my son off, hugged him goodbye and told him I'd see him in ten days. He wasn't happy hearing that, and told me it was too long, but I assured him I'd call him every evening before he went to bed. He put his head down and said okay, then turned and waved at me as he headed for the front door. "I love you, Dad!"

"I love you too, buddy, I'll call you later tonight."

It was always hard to leave my loved ones, but duty called, and I jumped on the road, making the five-hour drive back to the house that filled me with both dread and excitement. As soon as I stepped on the porch at 46 Welles Street, the door swung open, and James was there to greet me. "Man, am I glad to see you!" I walked into the house to find Jerry coming down the stairs with a young girl. She had jet-black hair and quite a few tattoos and piercings. Jerry welcomed me back with a bro hug and introduced me to Bambi. I bought my gear in and we all sat down in the living room to chat.

They proceeded to tell me they had just done a Ouija board session in the small room upstairs where a young man had reportedly committed suicide by a shotgun blast to his head. They all said they'd had some crazy responses, and damned if Jerry didn't ask me again if I would do a session with the board. I just gave him a look and he laughed. He knew it irritated me every time he asked me to use it. I told them they were nuts using the board again after what had happened the night before. Jerry smiled and said, "You know me, man, I push the limits."

"Yeah, you do," I said, "and one day it's going to bite you in the ass big time."

Jerry then announced that he and Bambi were going to do another Ouija board session, this time in the middle room, and James and I could film it and be there for back-up in case anything happened. We gathered our gear and went upstairs to set up. I placed a Mel Meter right on the table the Ouija board was on and lit two candles. I placed a Rem pod in the doorway that led to the old part of the house. I then sat down on the bed with a camera, facing the table. James also had a camera and was set up right in front where he could capture responses from the board.

Jerry opened the session with "Spirits of this house, we invite you to communicate with us by moving this planchette over the letters on this board. You can also use my energy to transmit any messages that you wish to get through. After the session is closed, and the planchette goes over to goodbye, then you have to leave. Is this understood?"

Nothing happened and Jerry repeated the question. There was still no movement. Bambi then asked if anyone was with us and the Mel Meter's temperature sensor went off as if a spirit was confirming its presence. Jerry asked who was there but again, there was no response until Bambi chimed in and asked the question. The planchette started moving very slowly and went to the letter M. It continued to move slowly around the board, spelling out the name Mary.

"Is your name Mary?" Bambi asked. The planchette started moving again, going to a series of letters starting with S. As this was happening, the Mel Meter went off again. The board completed spelling the word "sodomy." Bambi was taken aback and said "Oh, shit. That was a vulgar thing to say, why did you say that?" In response to her question, the planchette started moving around the board again. This time it spelled out "virgin."

Bambi asked if the reference was to the Virgin Mary and the planchette moved to the yes sign. This was all very upsetting to me because the feeling I was getting was something evil in nature was saying it wanted to sodomize the Virgin Mary.

Bambi said, "I don't think you are who you say you are." Again, the Mel Meter temperature sensor started going off, signaling another drop. At that moment, Bambi said she felt like her arm was being touched. She said it again, and the Mel Meter's audible alarm screamed out. The temperature dropped two more degrees to 67. At the same time, Jerry started having facial contortions and started fidgeting with his face, saying he suddenly had a massive headache. Bambi said, "Are you affecting Jerry right now?"

The planchette circled and went to yes. Bambi told Jerry to focus on the board so they could get more answers, and the planchette shot over to no. She asked the spirit again to identify itself. The Mel Meter continued to signal temperature drops while the planchette moved around the board. This time it spelled out the word demon. There was a pause and Bambi asked if anyone was still there. The planchette started to move and twist in a weird, almost sideways fashion. "I don't think that's a good sign when it does that," Bambi said. The planchette moved over to yes as if it was agreeing with her statement.

While this was going on, I was hearing noises in the room directly behind me, and I let everyone know. We could all feel the energy in the room; it was really escalating, and it felt negative in nature. Bambi continued to insist that the spirit tell us who it really was. The next sequence made absolutely no sense as it spelled out "dirst." It wasn't even a word. It was as if something was playing with us, showing us it could do what it wanted. Bambi asked the spirit if it thought it was God and the planchette spelled out the response: "I am." Again, the device started moving in an erratic fashion all over the board. It wasn't even stopping on any letters. We realized the communication was probably over.

Suddenly, there was a loud bang and I felt as if something came up through the floor and hit the bed right under where I was sitting. It hit with such force I was lifted up a bit. I sprang to my feet and yelled out. Everyone went into a frenzy, asking me if I had made the bang sound. As I was explaining what had just happened, there was a loud growl from the room behind me. The same room I had been hearing strange noises from earlier during the session. Bambi called out that there were more letters being spelled out on the board. You could hear the fright in her voice, and she was physically shaking as the planchette continued to move.

The room got chaotic. I scrambled to try to debunk the bang and what I felt as Jerry and Bambi kept going with the Ouija board session. "I am here" was spelled out on the board. Something was still in the room with us. Bambi cried out that her arm felt as if it was burning. Jerry was still being affected, too. His face looked different, and he kept wiping it. We decided to end the session since things were getting so negative.

An hour later, Jerry wanted to do another session with the Ouija board in the same room. Before I could respond, Bambi let out a scream from over by the stairs. We rushed over to find her standing there holding her purse and asked her what had happened.

"I bent over to grab my purse and the whole stair rail just shook violently. And you guys were nowhere around it anywhere."

I could tell she was really shaken up. Jerry and James came in with a camera rolling, and Bambi explained what had happened. We then proceeded upstairs, and Jerry opened the Ouija board session as usual, telling the spirits to come and communicate with him and Bambi. This time they placed a scrying mirror and a candle directly between them.

They put the Ouija board on their knees, so the mirror was under it, then they placed a ghost box right on the board. Bambi said, "We are going to do another session; can you communicate with us again?" The spirit box said, "Ouija board."

I was blown away because this showed an intelligent response to what they were doing. Bambi continued, telling the spirits they had to leave once the session was closed. Again, there was a response from the ghost box, this time it spat out "we're good." They put the box down and placed their hands on the planchette. Bambi started by asking who was there. "I can feel your energy entering the room, can you tell us who is here with us?"

The Mel Meter alarm went off and the planchette moved to spell out the word "evil." It then went to the number 6. When Bambi asked what this meant, the board moved to spell "go." Bambi asked if this meant that we were being told to go, to which the board moved to no. It was all rather erratic, so Bambi switched gears and again asked for a name. The planchette rapidly went to no. "I'm not asking you; I'm telling you now to tell me your name," demanded Bambi. Her demand resulted in the planchette spelling out "am Jerry."

Things were getting crazy in the room again. The hair on my arms and the back of my neck were standing up and the Mel Meter was going crazy. On the board, the planchette kept going to the same things, the number 6, the word no, and it kept spelling out "Jerry." Bambi was getting frustrated, she demanded in the name of God that the spirit reveal its name. She asked it why it wanted Jerry and if it had a message for them. The planchette spelled out "look" and "go now."

At that exact moment, I realized my eyes were burning and it smelled like smoke in the room. James and Bambi both noticed it, too. I got up to go downstairs and see if there was an issue with the wood burning stove. As soon as I opened the bedroom door, smoke poured into the room. I scrambled down the steps to discover the whole downstairs was full of smoke. I ran over to the stove and found the chimney flue was 3/4 of the way closed. It didn't make any sense. James and I had checked on the stove and put another log on the fire just before we all went upstairs. The flue was very stiff and difficult to operate, and we certainly would have noticed if it had been closed.

It was obvious to me something unseen had physically turned the flue until it was almost closed to either show us it could hurt us, or worse, to try to hurt us.

All of us were unnerved by the event. It took a while to air the house out, and needless to say, we were finished for the night. Clearly, whatever negative force was in the place wanted to cause us harm.

Day 10

The activity in the Welles house had been steadily increasing since the first day we arrived. It felt to me as if the house was actually feeding off of our energy, fears, and individual weaknesses. On a personal level, I was dealing with constant threats from my wife—now a daily occurrence. The rest of the team were experiencing a range of issues from business and financial problems to personal relationship issues. Everything seemed to be escalating in a very negative manner mentally, physically, and spiritually. Nevertheless, we all decided to continue and to attack the negative energies head on. We were determined not to let it get the best of us.

We decided to start the night with Bambi and me going upstairs to the back room where I had been hearing all the strange noises. We wanted to use a ghost box to see if we could make contact with whatever was causing the disturbances. James followed along with a camera running. Bambi turned the box on as we were climbing the stairs, and right away the word "burn" came from the box. I thought this was creepy since the whole house had filled with smoke just the night before. Was this the spirit telling us it wanted us to burn?

When we got in the room, the box blurted out the number six, along with the words "fight," and "fortunate." It was as if something was telling us we had been lucky to get out the night before. I already felt uneasy, and we had just started the investigation. I let Bambi keep running the box. We were already getting intelligent responses, even though we hadn't started asking questions. Bambi went after the spirit's name again and the box replied, "destroyer." The camera we had running immediately started pixelating out. This lasted for about five seconds. It was as if there were some strong, electromagnetic interference in the room.

Bambi announced she was holding the ghost box so they could communicate, and they could use her energy. A female voice came out of the box saying, "I hate it."

James said, "We went and got a huge bottle of holy water for you today, what do you think about that?" A raspy voice spat out of the ghost box, saying "Lucifer's family." Again, it was a direct, negative response in reaction to James's taunting about the holy water. It sent shivers down my spine.

Bambi started asking what was meant by "Lucifer's family," and right away, the camera pixelated out again. Clearly something was interfering with our equipment. Bambi asked, "Do you want us to spray and bless the whole house with holy water?"

"I don't," said a voice from the box.

Bambi told us she felt really nervous in the room. She asked the spirits again who owned the house and again, there was a creepy response. "Death." Bambi asked the spirits if they were trying to scare us, and the raspy voice responded "surround."

Every response unnerved us more at this point. James jumped in with a question: "Did you try to burn the house down last night, when the house filled with smoke?"

"Yeah," came the quick response.

Bambi asked what the spirits were trying to do to us, and the box replied "offering." Then the number six came out of the box again. We still weren't sure what the relevance of the number was, but Bambi asked, "Do six people need to die to please you?"

"Exactly," said the voice.

We ended the session so we could discuss the responses we were getting. Since there were obvious threats against our lives, we decided to use some provoking techniques. Jerry brought the Dybbuk box upstairs to use in the middle room. We knew that a number of Jewish families had lived in the house over the years so we thought the box would upset any negative spirits in the home. On one level I didn't agree with using the box, but at the same time I was interested to see if using it would elicit any kind of response.

Jerry took out the various items contained in the box: an old black and white picture of a woman, a candle and candle holder, a small plate, and a lace doily, some red human hair, and what looked like a wedding band. Jerry asked out loud why the place was a house of death. I heard what sounded like a very faint whistle, followed by numerous whispering voices. The words were not distinguishable. Jerry confirmed he'd heard the same thing. He told the spirits to speak louder so we could hear them. Again, the faint talking started. We were all in the room together, so we knew it wasn't anyone on the team. Out of nowhere, there was a strong smell of sulfur in the room. It became so bad we had to cover our mouths and noses with our shirts to keep from gagging and puking. Jerry then started to ramp things up, saying, "If you don't like this Dybbuk box being in here, move one of the items, throw one across the room, show us you don't like it." Cameras rolling, we waited for a response, but there was nothing. Jerry started calling out various demonic names. This made me extremely uncomfortable. After five more minutes of no activity, Jerry turned on the Jewish prayers and asked if the spirits liked the word of God being spoken in the home. We heard a sound like the dragging of furniture. It was coming out of the same room we had heard the other strange sounds from the night before.

Jerry headed into the back room, trying to figure out what caused the sound. I stood in the doorway with the camera rolling, but we found nothing out of place. We resumed our positions around the items from the Dybbuk box, and Jerry continued to ask questions. After a moment, we heard the dragging sound once again. I swung the camera around quickly, but there was nothing there. The Jewish prayers were still playing and just then, I heard a disembodied voice scream out. It sounded like something was very angry. We later verified that the weird scream was captured on the camera's audio. There was no further activity, so we regrouped. James went to the middle room and turned on a ghost box, stating, "I want answers! Can you tell me what I have in my hand?"

This time "Beelzebub" came across the box. James pulled out a pocketknife and asked what he had in his hand. The box responded "sharp…knife."

"It's a hunting knife and it's no joke," James replied. "What would you do if you had it?" This time, the box gave a chilling, specific reply: "Attack each one of you."

I was getting angry because an entity had now threatened us yet again. There were no more responses to questions, and we were just about to wrap up the session when James spotted a couple of flashes coming from the back room. We investigated but couldn't find anything to explain the weird lights. At this point, the Mel Meter on the back stairs started to go off. James turned on the ghost box and asked, "Is that you making this device go off?" A female voice responded yes.

James started interacting, asking for the meter to go off at specific times, and it did. After several moments of interaction, the activity again ceased. We would later learn the static camera in the room had picked up numerous flashes of light. These flashes could not be detected with the naked eye, but our full spectrum cameras registered them.

With no further activity, we moved to the stairway and again, the area registered a high reading of EMF coming in at 9.5 mG on the meter. We used a different ghost box and asked why the spirit was staying in the abandoned house.

"Cannot leave," it said. We asked what kind of rituals had been performed in the home and received the words "black magic."

With the term black magic coming out of the box, something from the history of the home came to my mind. One of the families that previously lived in the house had discovered items related to the practice of Voodoo. A Voodoo doll had been found buried under the back stairwell of the home. There was also another strange item found. The home had an old fireplace that was once used for cooking. In it was discovered an old tin box containing human hair wrapped around chicken bones. All these items were found in the section of the house that had originally been servant quarters.

We wrapped up the session and went to take a brief break. Checking my phone, I found that once again, I had numerous text messages from my wife telling me she was being attacked in her sleep by something evil. I texted her back and tried calling her several times but there was no response. I chalked it up to it being late, figuring she had fallen back asleep. Continuing our investigation, we went back up to the hell room. I placed a Mel Meter in front of a big mirror leaning against one of the walls. The meter was at zero and I asked if there was a spirit in the mirror. Immediately, the gauge went to .03 mG. I then asked, "Do you use mirrors to travel?" The EMF readout shot up to 1.6 mG and the temperature readout went to 66.6. Obviously, something was mocking the Holy Trinity by displaying the number 666 to us.

Jerry, who was running the camera, announced he was feeling

sick, and I began to feel dizzy. We were both being physically affected by something. "If you're making me dizzy, make the device light up again," I said. As soon as I had the words out, the device lit up. I started cussing at the entity, agitated that we were being affected in such a way. I picked up a ball in the room and shouted, "Knock this damn ball out of my hand!"

The meter lit up again, and I was getting more and more agitated. I kept prodding the entity to do something. I even pulled out my tactical knife and said, "Do you want me to cut myself?" As my aggravation increased, I became more belligerent toward the negative entity. I grabbed the ghost box and turned it on and said "We're gonna burn this damn house down."

"Yeah" came the response from the box. Whatever was in the house was enjoying my agitation. I should add here that this behavior is totally out of character for me. I am usually very level-headed and scientific in my approach during any investigation. On this occasion, however, I was being manipulated by something negative in nature, and it was in turn feeding off the negative energy I was putting out.

The box spit out "I'm leaving" and Jerry quickly asked where to. Again, there was an intelligent response from the box, and it said, "back porch."

I was still agitated, and I started jumping up and down saying, "I am gonna burn this mother fucker down! What are you gonna do about it?" "Burn it" was the reply.

Jerry and I both heard a growl coming from the back room. The ghost box said "danger" as if trying to warn us. Then another series of words started coming from the box. "Beezle.... Satan." My agitation was still growing, and I was pounding on a small shelf in the room. Jerry finally said we were ending the session because something was having too much of an effect on me. When we went downstairs, all the anger suddenly went away. I was completely exhausted, both physically and mentally. We ended the night's work, and I went quickly to sleep.

Day 11

A curious pattern emerged at the Welles house. Each night we would start with a basic sweep to determine EMF levels in the house. On nights that the EMF readings were low, there would be a higher level of activity in the house. On nights when the readings were high, activity would be lower. My thirty years in the field has almost always shown the opposite to be true. It was puzzling and I scratch my head about it to this day, but nothing is sure in the paranormal. It's possible the entities in the house were utilizing the EMF energy to manifest, hence the lower readings.

We continued our investigation in the oldest section of the house. The temperature dropped five degrees right away and I tried some EVP sessions. During this time, there was a white light anomaly picked up by the cameras. It was about the size of a volleyball and it came out of the Mel Meter and moved vertically. This happened just as the temperature sensor lit up on the Mel Meter. I turned on a ghost box and received a flurry of words including help, no and leave.

The temperature sensor was going nuts and I asked who was making it get colder. There was a response of "I am...that was me." I announced that I was going to go up into the attic of the house. Something didn't like the idea because my statement caused the box to respond, "punch him, blood."

Jerry, James, and I had gone into the attic earlier in the day, looking for any possible artifacts to use as trigger objects. I asked the box who had gone into the attic before and it answered, "hold on... three." Obviously, something was watching us at all times in the house. I asked how many spirits were with us and the answer was, "there's a couple here."

We were sitting in a room where one wall was covered with a wood panel. Years earlier, there had been a fire in the house and the panel was covering evidence of the fire. It was also the same wall that connected to the stairwell where the Voodoo doll had been discovered. I pointed at the panel and announced, "I'm going to tear this wall down." The response from the box was, "maybe you should."

I changed tactics a bit and said, "We are going to bring a priest and a monk in tomorrow to bless this house. How do you feel about that?" This comment brought responses of "no" and "the devil" from the box. Just then we heard a growl followed by a hissing sound. The sounds were not from the ghost box, but rather from something in the room. They were so loud we jumped back and looked at each other for confirmation. The ghost box then said the word "hiss." The level of interaction was uncanny. As we were puzzling over this, the box stated "David, listen."

"Who just said my name?"

"Beelzebub" came the reply.

James and I were getting cold chills. The hair on our arms stood up and we started hearing noises coming from the middle room behind us. James started reciting a prayer and it angered something because the box spit out "don't do it, stop" and "too late." But it didn't stop there. We also heard screams of pain, growls, and more threatening comments like get out and be careful. This all further affirmed to me there was something evil in the Welles house. I decided to end the session but asked one final question:

"What is in my pocket right now?"

The response came quickly, "nothing."

It was the correct answer. How could a spirit or entity know what was in my pocket at that moment?

We moved the investigation to the stairwell. A quick EMF reading showed a level of 10.4 mG, a pretty high reading. I started an EVP session and right away, I had an extremely bad headache. It came on me out of nowhere. I thought it may be due to the high EMF levels, but it was so overwhelming I had to stop the session and exit the house to get some relief. After spending about twenty minutes outside, the headache completely went away.

The Mel Meter on the steps was going crazy. We put a second one near it to verify there wasn't any kind of malfunction with the equipment, and both meters became active. Additionally, the 360-degree static meter we had on the steps began to react to something. It was incredible to witness three pieces of equipment all being manipulated at the same time. Clearly there was much more to come from the Welles house.

Day 12

It was Halloween.

We were all drained of energy even though we had slept decently for once. All day long and into the night, cars were pulling up in front of the house and people were standing outside taking pictures. There were kids and adults alike, many in costume, taking photos. It was like a zoo with us as the featured exhibit.

Word was out that a paranormal team was at the Welles house, and since it was Halloween, folks wanted to come out and see what was happening. It was annoying, but at the same time a bit exciting to be part of something so significant.

When it came time to begin our investigation, we conducted several EVP sessions in various parts of the house. No responses were recorded. The night was off to a slow start. Things started getting active when James and Bambi conducted a ghost box session in the middle room. It always seemed to be an area of high activity, and as soon as the box was on, it said "red" and "Beezle."

James started interacting with something that said it was behind him. He began to demand that the entity stop hiding and come out of the corner. He sprayed holy water into the corner to which the ghost box said "bad." James continued to call the entity out until the box finally said, "I'm here."

"Yes, that's what we want." James replied. "Now do something, anything you can to communicate with us. Knock that chair over, push that ladder down, slam the door. Anything you can do to let us know you're here, do it now. I'm just going to start spraying holy water." The response from the box was "please don't."

It was crazy. What kind of ghost or entity would say please don't? It didn't seem like it could be the same negative force we had been dealing with. James started threatening to spray the whole room down and the voices from the box suddenly turned negative, issuing a series of comments including "get out…leave…fuck you!"

James was spraying holy water all around, provoking the entity to speak to us. Bambi chimed in and asked, "Do you want us to light this candle?" Again, there was a flurry of responses. "You whore…be careful…shitty candle."

James asked if he'd get attacked if he lit the candle. "Don't light it...you'll find out," came the response.

Of course, James lit the candle. From the ghost box came a scream of pain unlike anything I had ever heard come from a spirit box. It sent shivers down my spine and James and Bambi were both visibly shaken by the sound.

"Devil," said the box as James reached over and shut it off. He picked up a recorder and did an EVP session. Again, we told the spirits we would be bringing in a priest to bless the house. On playback, we received a class A EVP that said, "You better not." We moved into the back room of the house and James continued spraying holy water all around. Bambi turned on the ghost box and started right off by saying, "Do you like the holy water? That's just the start."

A nasty voice from the box answered her with "leave tramp."

Bambi took the holy water from James and started to spray it all around. James held the ghost box and asked for the name of the people who had conjured the negative entity. The name of a family that had lived in the house was given. Bambi fired off more questions, asking the entity if something had been hidden in the fireplace, if it was a ritualistic item. The box responded to each question. "One time." "Spiritual."

Bambi told us something was touching her arm and at the same moment, James reported that it felt as if something physically moved the ghost box in his hand. I had been feeling as if something was all around me during their session but didn't say anything until they too reported their interactions. While we were discussing this, there was a loud, wheezing growl in the room. We all heard the sound, and it hadn't come from the ghost box. Next, there was a loud bang followed by footsteps. We assumed it was Jerry moving around downstairs, so we called down to ask him. There was no response, and we called down to him several more times, but there was still no answer. I rushed downstairs only to discover Jerry was outside smoking a cigarette. I asked him if he'd just gone out, and he said he'd been outside behind the house on his phone during our entire session. I couldn't believe it; it was a clear demonstration of more physical manifestations from whatever was in the house.

I went back upstairs and filled the rest of the team in. We continued with our session. It was then I felt I became the main target of the negative entity. It started with the feeling of a negative presence all around me. I told James and Bambi this was happening. James turned on the ghost box while Bambi started spraying holy water again. A flurry of threatening comments came out of the box. "That's your best? Dave...we're gonna get him. Trouble in the attic."

Bambi, with holy water in hand, asked if they were afraid of her and a resounding "No!" came through clearly.

"Help me to kill Dave," came out of the box. Right away, I told Bambi to start spraying me with the holy water, hoping it would offer some protection from the threats that were coming in. "I just sprayed Dave with holy water, you can't bother him anymore." The voice from the box came back with, "Fucker! I don't care."

James started getting freaked out and asked me if I kicked the couch. I told him I hadn't even moved. He was insistent that something had moved the sofa. There was a loud exhale from right behind me. I swung the camera around, hoping to catch some activity and as I did, the box said, "get Dave." I was unnerved by all that was happening, and I started saying prayers of protection. Jerry came up and wanted to get in on the session. He suggested using the Ouija board again.

Considering all the negative energy flying around me, I didn't even want to be in the room while he conducted a session with the board, so I headed downstairs and went outside. I needed to be out of the house for a bit.

I don't know what transpired during the session they did with the Ouija board. I do know that when I later saw Jerry come downstairs, he didn't look right. He looked sort of like he was in a trance. Of course, I can only imagine how I looked after coming out of that room and the intense energy it held. We all took a long break before trying any more sessions.

After the break James and I went upstairs and turned on a spirit device. Right away the negativity started again with the device spitting out, "It's going to get Spinks scratched" and "help me get them."

James asked the entity what it thought about God and the responses were "fool...fuck you." James asked if the ritual used to conjure the spirit could be undone. "Only with fire" came the response. That reply further connected with information we had just received.

Earlier in the day we had spoken with an individual who told us that at one point, a psychic had been brought in and asked what could be done about the negativity. The psychic's dramatic reply was that the entire house needed to be burned to the ground in order to cleanse the property of the evil that existed there.

While we were playing back the recorder, checking for responses, we heard three distinct knocks followed by a signal from the temperature gauge noting a .5 degree drop. I then had a brief, disturbing set of responses from questions directed to the ghost box.

"Was the person that brought you here a witch?"

"Yes…black arts."

"Did that person use black magic?"

"Yes…black arts…in her house."

We went downstairs and took a quick break before our next session. This time the guys wanted to try something a bit more intense as a trigger. James had brought along a priest outfit. He intended to put it on and walk around the house, blessing each room with holy water. I felt it was a dangerous tactic and said so. Since James wasn't an actual priest, I felt it could backfire on him and he could become the target for a severe attack by a negative entity. It would also leave the rest of us open to more attacks if something had a strong reaction to the tactic.

In spite of my concerns, I had to acknowledge that I had signed on for such things as a paranormal investigator. These kinds of experiments were all part of the process of trying to understand what we were dealing with. Besides, I wasn't going to leave these guys since I had committed to backing them up.

James got dressed in his priest attire and started walking through the house spraying holy water. Jerry followed with a camera and I walked along with a digital recorder. When the two of them reached the top of the steps, Jerry stopped and said he'd heard a loud hiss. Neither James nor I heard it, but on playback it was clear on the audio recorder, and it occurred just as James commanded the entity to show itself.

We continued through the rooms. When we reached the back bedroom, Jerry reported that something touched his neck three times in quick succession. Meanwhile, James announced that he was waylaid and almost fell down. He kept repeating, "You cannot touch me, I am protected by God. Show us where you are, right now." He reported seeing a shadow figure behind me. The meters were going off, both in the room with us and in the next bedroom.

"We are going to bless every inch of this house. If you don't like it, show us."

We then heard two distinct knocks on the wall near us and the infrared light battery went dead on the camera. I went over to reset the Mel Meter because it was still going off, and I wanted to rule out any malfunction. James said, "If we are making you mad, set the meter off again." It took all of three seconds for the meter to go off once again.

The energy in the room felt charged and negative. James said he felt as if the room were spinning and he became dizzy. He continued spraying holy water, but the activity in the room suddenly stopped. We tried a few more tactics, but there was nothing else happening, so we called it a night.

Halloween had produced a flurry of activity in the house, and then, there was complete stillness.

Day 13

We started off in the back bedroom with EMF detectors placed strategically around the room, one at the center and one at the back stairs. Countless times during our investigations in the house, we had received the number six on audio devices, and I wanted to try to get to the bottom of its meaning. As soon as Bambi turned on a ghost box, I asked who six was. "Demons" came the reply.

"Who is hiding in this house" I asked. This time, the ghost box spat out the name "Azrael." This was an interesting response, since Azrael is the angel of death and there had been a lot of death on the property. As I was thinking about this, the box suddenly said, "Get out Bambi." Things were turning negative very quickly and we were already on edge. Bambi asked if something was hiding in the corner and the response was "one." When I asked who the one was and who was hiding in the house, the replies were "six" and "the girl."

Again, it seemed something was toying with us and being cryptic in its responses. I started to feel like something was touching me once again and the box confirmed this suspicion by saying "yeah" and

"Beezle." Bambi told us she felt like something was sticking a finger in her eyes, and her eyes started burning.

I asked the box, "Do you want us to come up into the attic tonight?"

"Hurt you…Spinks," it replied.

Again, something was calling my name and threatening me. I said, "We're going to spray a bunch of holy water in here tonight, what do you think about that?"

"Demonic," the voice replied.

I asked the voice to confirm if it was demonic and the response was, "I am."

Growls and hissing noises started coming out of the ghost box. The energy in the house felt off the charts. We moved our investigation to the main stairwell, one of the proven hotspots, and tried a few different things. EVP burst sessions and attempts to get a knocking response resulted in nothing but silence. After the dramatic amount of activity, the house suddenly seemed very quiet. I finally pulled out an old hack shack ghost box. The device was one of my favorite things to use during the Welles house investigation. I started with a very different question, asking, "Do you miss your mommy?" I thought if there were any spirits of children in the house, this might call them forward. The box gave a response of yes and Bambi asked, "What drove you to kill yourself?" "Bottle," came the reply.

While this clearly wasn't a child's spirit, it was compelling nonetheless because there had been numerous reports of alcohol and drug abuse in the home's history. So many cases of abuse could be linked in some way to the presence of negative entities in the house. Perhaps these entities had been exerting some kind of control over these people, driving them to substance abuse and making them weaker and weaker in order to possess them.

As we continued asking questions pertaining to people who had committed suicide in the house, the ghost box kept shutting off. I couldn't help but wonder if this too was a negative entity, not wanting us to discover more information about the human spirits in the home. I asked if one of the human spirits in the home had been attacked by something they couldn't see, and there was an immediate response of "yes."

I then asked if one of the spirits had abused drugs, and again received a response of yes. There were some minor spikes on the Mel Meter, and I continued with more questions. I asked the spirit, "How old were you when you died?" "Fourteen," it responded.

We were aware a teenage boy had committed suicide in the house, but we were never able to verify his age. Was this his spirit? Unfortunately, there was no further information during the session.

Jerry and I decided to go up to the room where the boy had shot himself to see if we could get further responses from any of the suicide victims. There were other reports claiming that at least two people had hanged themselves in the house, so Jerry fashioned a makeshift noose out of some clothesline as a trigger object. He started off with the questions and had an exchange with what seemed to be the spirit of one of the people who had killed themselves. "We want to talk to the person who supposedly hanged themselves in this room."

The voice coming over the spirit box claimed it was the spirit of someone who had hanged themselves in the basement. When Jerry placed the rope around his own neck, a range of excited voices came forth with comments like "hang him" and "kill," followed by laughter.

Jerry took the rope off and hung it from the bedroom door, telling the spirits to move the rope if they could. He told me he felt weird in the room, as if there were a static charge in the air. We heard the Mel Meter down on the dining room table going off, so we ran down to see what was occurring. Jerry asked out loud if a spirit had been touching the meter. On cue, the device went off again. There was a brief exchange with various pieces of equipment going off, but no further evidence came forth, so we decided to take a break.

I stepped outside to get some air. Pulling out my cell phone, I discovered I had over thirty missed calls. All of them were from my wife. I had already spoken to her earlier that day, and she knew I would be investigating and out of reach. I called her back and when she answered, the exchange was not a pleasant one. I asked right away if everything was all right, and she gave a curt reply of "no."

"What's wrong now?"

"I'm moving out."

"What? Really?"

"Yes."

"If that's what you want to do then do it."

This had been building for a while and I'd had enough. We argued for a bit and I told her that giving me an ultimatum was not going to work for me. I explained, again, that she already knew I was an investigator, and I wasn't going to stop because she had a problem with it. She couldn't believe I would choose the paranormal over being with her and this threw her into another tirade. She kept going on and on, and finally I just hung up on her and turned my phone to silent. I knew she wouldn't hear anything I had to say. The whole mess had started two days into the investigation of the Welles house, and I figured it all was just another ploy to try to get me to quit and go home sooner. Once back in the house, everyone started asking if I was all right. No doubt, they'd heard the yelling coming out of my cell phone even in the house. I brushed it off telling them I was fine. I didn't want to get into the whole thing and there was more work to be done.

We moved to the main stairwell again to try some more sessions. Jerry started asking questions and a series of responses came from the ghost box including demons, six, and this time, the number three. Jerry switched gears and asked if there was a succubus in the house. There was no response, so he changed up the question a bit. "Do you want to have sex with one of the humans in this house?" The response was yes. When Jerry asked who the spirit wanted, the response was clear: "Dave."

"Do you want Dave to go up into the hell room right now?"

"Uh Huh."

Right away Jerry was ready to use me for shark bait or a human trigger object. I went up to the hell room and lay down on the bed with a REM pod between my legs. (The REM pod detects ambient temperature changes and disturbances in the EMF field.) I was left upstairs by myself. The cameras were running and so was the ghost box. I was hoping to catch further evidence to back up what we'd heard on the stairs.

"You can touch one of the devices, but you can't touch or hurt me," I stated.

I was really uncomfortable with being bait in such an experiment. I was on edge and felt like something may attack me any second. "I'm up here now, what do you want? Do you like to hurt men?"

A clear female voice came out of the ghost box and said yes. I was even more spooked, so I sat up on the bed and tried to continue the dialogue. "Why do you like to hurt men?" The voice responded, "Don't worry about it."

At that moment, the camera caught some strange shadow movement at the foot of the bed. It looked like something trying to manifest. As this was occurring, I felt the bed shake. I asked if a spirit had shaken the bed and the response was yes.

My guard was up even more now. This activity was occurring in the same bed I had tried to sleep in my first night at the house. I started seeing strange light flashes in the corner of the room, and then the bed shook again. I was describing the sensation for the camera when I felt something grab my right leg. Of course, I jumped in reaction. Right as this was happening, a voice from the ghost box told me to go to sleep.

I would later learn that numerous light anomalies were being captured on film while all of this was happening. There was also an unexplainable white mist captured in the room while I was in there.

I felt another touch, this time on my left arm at the same time as the phrase "grab him" came out of the ghost box. The camera also captured a strange white light that moved from my arm in an upward direction. A woman's voice came over the spirit box and said "kill."

"Who do you want to kill?" I asked. "You," came the chilling response.

I asked if I was speaking to the same entity that had hurt me previously and why it wanted to kill me. "We are. We are waiting for you," came the response.

It was disturbing to note that whatever was communicating at this point was referring to itself in the plural. Clearly, this was not a human spirit.

The box stated my name again and it felt like something started playing with my hair. A woman's voice came through and told me that my time was up.

"My time's up when I say it's up," I replied. I felt what I can only describe as a hand being placed on my back. I jumped up out of the bed. It took me a few moments to regain my composure and then I got back on the bed and continued the dialogue. "So, I'm the guinea pig here. Are you the one that attacked me the other night and made me throw up?"

"Yep."

I asked again for the spirit to name itself and as I did, I felt something touch my head. I stated that I was only going to remain in the room a few more minutes and that if the spirit had anything to tell me, it had better do so. What followed was a series of foul, sexual responses. "Dick" came over the ghost box and I asked the entity if it liked to rape men. "Yes, all of them," was the response.

"Why do you like to attack men?"

"Pain…rape."

"You like to rape men; how many men have you hurt or killed in this house?"

"Yeah…killed five."

"So, you've killed five men in this house?"

"Yes."

"Wow…that's crazy. I'm not going to be number six." I started to feel hot, almost to the point of sweating and asked, "Are you trying to touch me?"

"Yes, I am."

I started to feel very nauseated. Two separate voices came across the box and both said the word blood. The bed shook once again and a voice from the box asked, "Do you want to be used?"

"No, I do not want to be used." I became light-headed and the physical symptoms I was experiencing prompted me to ask, "Are you trying to weaken me so you can attack me?"

"Of course. I'm having fun."

"My time is about done here. I've had enough of this bullshit. Do you want me to leave?"

"You won't do that."

"Watch me!" I immediately ended the session. On later review of the camera footage, I was blown away by all the various light anomalies that had occurred during my time in the bedroom. There were different unexplained lights throughout the session and many of them were timed with various responses and sensations I had during the interaction with whatever was coming through. It remains one of the most compelling sessions I've ever experienced in my entire investigative career.

After my time in the hell room, we checked out the attic. Once we were up there, I noticed a small opening in the back wall. I peered through and saw it opened to a huge attic space over the newest part of the house. Inside I saw what appeared to be three old wooden barrels. I decided to go back down and up through the other attic entrance, so I could gain access to that side and check out the barrels. They turned out to be old nail barrels. They were all empty and there didn't seem to be anything significant about them, but I brought one down so everyone could check it out.

Bambi decided to go up to the hell room and conduct a session herself. She wanted to see what kind of responses she could get since it had been so active around me. She used an SB-7 spirit box and began with, "I'm here to speak with the succubus tonight, are you here with me?" "I am," came the response.

"I want you to tell me your name, very clearly through the box."

"David."

"Are you the one that has been attacking the men in this house?"

"Be careful."

"I want you to tell me, are you a demon?"

"I am."

Bambi felt like something was touching her arm and asked, "Are you touching me right now?"

"Yes."

Bambi took off her rosary and announced she now had no protection and for them to talk to her. Just as she finished saying this, the spirit box went nuts and started spewing all kinds of growls, hisses, and inaudible words. Bambi asked again if there was a succubus in the house. "You slut, go hide," the voice responded.

"I want you to scratch me or knock something over," Bambi stated.

"Bathroom."

Again, a wide range of sounds began coming out of the box, weird screams, moans, growls, and unusual electronic sputtering. It was so bizarre, like sounds coming from Hell itself, and the whole thing was rather unnerving to watch on the live feed, with Bambi upstairs alone. If something happened, it would take us several seconds to get up to her. She continued challenging the entity to do something to prove it was present. A female voice came out of the box and said, "get her."

"Where in this house do you like to hide?"

"In the stairs."

Bambi said something then grabbed her leg. Moments later, she jumped and the floor beneath her feet popped loudly, and she could feel movement. The Ovilus, which had been silent, suddenly said "mommy." Immediately afterward the SB-7 also said "mommy" three consecutive times. It's always compelling when multiple devices provide the same information. Bambi said she felt like she was being touched all over. We wondered if this was a child spirit trying to make contact with her since she was female. Bambi soon ended the session and came back downstairs.

We wrapped up for the night and I sat thinking about the recent activity in the house. During Bambi's session, there were tons of things coming through the spirit box. My name was spoken multiple times, along with the words evil and demon. After my own experiences in the hell room, it was clear something was after me. I had to wonder to myself, why was I staying? But the answer came quickly. Despite everything that had happened, I still thirsted for more. Even though I had been physically and mentally affected numerous times in the house, I wanted and needed more. I knew it was affecting my personal life, but I could not pull myself away from it. The drive to document the activity was simply too strong.

Day 14

Jerry and Bambi were back at it with the Ouija board. As usual I refused to participate but stood by to help document anything that occurred. They set up as they had before and opened the session. The board spelled out the word "blood" and the alarms on the Mel Meters went off. There was an audible growl in the room and the board began to spell out a series of random words, none of which made any sense: tangle, tweet, and Plato.

Bambi asked about the wooden barrels we had found in the attic and the board spelled out "snake." She asked if snakes were kept in the barrels. The planchette moved, spelling out the word "bones." When Bambi asked if bones were kept in the barrels, the planchette quickly moved to yes. We did experience some additional growling noises and the sound of footsteps, but overall, this was one of our least eventful sessions in the house. We ended and went downstairs to take a break.

At three AM, we headed upstairs to investigate some more. We set up with the noose as a trigger object again, hoping to replicate the session we'd done the night before. As soon as Jerry turned the hack shack on, there was a deep growling "yeah" from it. Jerry repeated the "yeah" and said, "I like that sound." He then asked who had said yeah, and if they were still with us.

"You're gonna get it."

"What are you gonna do to me?"

There was no immediate response, but Jerry said the room felt charged up to him. I continued running the camera as he kicked things up a few notches. He slipped the noose around his neck and told the spirits he would help them out and they should pull on the rope.

"Tear your face off."

"Are you touching me?"

"Yes."

"How did you kill yourself?"

"Demonic."

"What is demonic?"

"Spirits."

"How did you die in this room?"

"Spirit…helped me do it."

Now, I found this incredibly disturbing. To think some spirit or entity had somehow helped someone kill themselves in the very room I was standing in was sickening. Jerry addressed the spirit of the person who had committed suicide and asked if they were sorry that they had killed themselves. A clear response of yes was heard. I was suddenly overwhelmed with feelings of deep sadness. I was so overcome I could feel tears welling up in my eyes. I'm not the emotional sort, so this was very unlike me. A loud scream of pain came out of the ghost box. Jerry said his arm was cold and came over and told me to touch it. He was correct, his arm was ice cold. I asked, "Who touched Jerry?"

"The Devil."

I was a bit shaken by all the energy and still fighting off the sadness. Jerry responded to the box with, "What other names does the Devil go by?"

"He has many."

A loud female voice came in and told Jerry it was going to kill him. He flew into a rage and started screaming at the box. "You wanna kill me…kill me!"

"I'll do it."

"Kill me you piece of shit…do it!" Jerry continued antagonizing the spirit, screaming right back at it. There were numerous negative responses coming from the box during this tirade, but nothing physical was happening. Jerry was still getting more and more pissed off. The tension was so thick in the room you could cut it with a knife. As he continued to provoke the spirit, a voice came across the box that said, "in your bed."

This simply added more fuel to Jerry's fire. He kept yelling at the entity to do it now.

"Chop you…tonight. Chop your head."

The provoking and screaming went on for a bit and finally Jerry ended the session. We went downstairs and switched off with James who went up to try to get more information. He asked a series of questions, asking who it was that wanted to hurt Jerry and asking to speak to the boy who had killed himself. When he asked if a spirit had helped people kill themselves in the house, the response was, "tormented them. Helped hang him."

It was more disturbing evidence to back up the things Jerry and I had heard. Reflecting back on the session Jerry and I had done in the room, my personal belief is that I witnessed something negative affect Jerry very deeply. It's difficult to spend so much time in such a negative location and not have it affect your life in some way. I've learned this from personal experience.

Day 15

It was time to take a break from the investigation so we could all go visit our families. The eight-hour drive back home flew by, and as always, once I was away from the Welles house, I felt much lighter and happier. Although I was looking forward to spending some time with my son, I was not happy knowing I was going to need to deal with my wife. I thought again about our conversation and her extreme reaction to my investigative work. I knew she was moving out, but somehow, I felt free and a bit more alive knowing I was going to be on my own once again, free to pursue my passion without being harassed on a constant basis.

I spent a few days with my son and soon received the call from Jerry that it was time to head back to the house. He told me James would no longer be part of the team.

James himself called me later to ask if I was going back to the house. I told him I was. He explained that he'd had a disagreement with Jerry and said he would never go back to the Welles house again. This wasn't too big a surprise to me after all the times James had almost left the investigation already.

James also gave me a stern warning about what he believed were the dangers of the house and how everyone investigating it was at risk. I told him I understood, but as risky and vile as the location was, I knew my mission there was not over, and I needed to collect more evidence.

Hanging up, I thought about what James had said, but I knew that something about the Welles house still had a hold on me and there was something I had to finish. During my time away from the house, it felt as if the place was calling me back. Practically all I could think about was getting back there and documenting more of the paranormal activity. My gear stayed packed in my truck and ready to go at any time. All I waited for was the call that everyone was good to go. When it finally came, I could hardly sleep the night before. In that state between sleep and waking, I had what I would call a dream, the same dream I'd had about James while I was in the house. There was the same demonic figure, standing there chanting and making weird hand and finger signs. The kicker was this time it wasn't James I saw the figure standing over. It was me.

Day 16

The eight-hour drive back to the Welles house was a weird mix of excitement and dread. I couldn't shake the image of the demon standing over me carrying on with whatever it was attempting. I took in the beautiful day as I parked and got out of my truck. I breathed in the crisp, fall air, and said a quick prayer as I climbed the steps to number 46. Jerry and Bambi met me at the door. They both looked well, and I could see they had already been busy unpacking gear. As soon as I crossed the threshold, the heaviness hit me as if the weight of the entire house was on my chest. I thought to myself, here we go again. By five o'clock we had all the gear unpacked, cameras set up and a fire going in the old wood stove.

We ran up to a local burger joint to get some food before the night's investigation. Looking at the menu, I was eyeballing a double burger with bacon and the works, when I suddenly remembered a psychic and witch friend of mine telling me I should never eat meat before an investigation, especially if I was going to a negative location. The evil spirits would be able to smell the blood from the meat, and it would draw them in. I only hesitated a moment. Time to test the theory, and soon a double, greasy burger with bacon and all the fixings was on its way to me.

Fueled up, back at the house, and ready to investigate, we encountered all kinds of electrical problems right off the bat. Brand new, fully charged batteries right out of the package were dead. We would put batteries in a piece of equipment and the charge would show full, but within a couple of minutes they would be completely drained. The battery situation was so bad, I ran down to a local store and bought a big supply of batteries, then left them in my truck in hopes they would be safe from the energy drain of the house. There were other electrical issues too. Lights in the house kept flickering and dimming on their own and we could find no explanation for it. Also, our live feed crashed, and we had to start a new one.

While all of this was occurring, the REM pod we had set up in the hell room was taking massive hits. No one was in the room, but the device was acting like someone or something had grabbed ahold of it. We also heard what sounded like several people upstairs, pacing back and forth through the bedrooms.

Jerry of course was raring to go with the Ouija board again. As usual, he and Bambi set up, this time in the middle bedroom, and opened the session. Right off, we started hearing strange scratching noises coming from the walls of the house. Jerry started asking questions and said he felt odd, as if all his energy were being drained. Bambi addressed the spirits with, "Are you draining Jerry's energy? Who are we talking to right now?" The planchette moved to "yes," then spelled out the word "coming."

Bambi asked if the spirit was one of the people who had committed suicide in the house. The response on the board was "are you." When Bambi began to ask for a name, the planchette moved around spelling out "Diablo." Obviously, it was another name for the devil. Bambi pushed this a little, asking the spirit if it really thought that it was the devil. The planchette began to move to each number on the board, as if it were counting down to something. When Bambi asked what the countdown was for, the planchette spelled out "Zengauare."

We later researched this word thoroughly but could find nothing. Perhaps it was a nonsensical response, or perhaps it is so obscure that any references are impossible to find. Bambi began to feel something touching her arm and the planchette spelled out "slut." Jerry suddenly freaked out, saying he was seeing things on the board and he broke contact with the planchette. Bambi quickly closed the session. Jerry was really unsettled. We asked him what he had seen, and his only reply was "a face."

He snatched the board back up, placed it on his and Bambi's knees and set a ghost box on it. Then he grabbed the picture of the woman out of the Dybbuk box and placed it on the board. He began to demand that the woman come and speak to him. There were a series of responses from the ghost box to his questions. Things like "kill them" and "it's here" issued forth. Jerry still seemed out of sorts. He reported being touched and started yelling for the spirits to attack him and kept trying to get some communication from the woman in the photograph.

Meanwhile, something was touching me on my back and my neck, and a loud boom came from somewhere in the house. Jerry turned off the ghost box, demanded the spirits move something in the room, then abruptly told me to sit down in a chair. He gave me the photo and a candle holder, both items from the Dybbuk box, took the camera I was holding and turned on the ghost box. Then he announced he was leaving me alone in the room because he believed the entities there would mess with me.

I was a bit out of sorts during all of this and tried to maintain my composure. When everyone was out of the room, I asked who the woman in the picture is.

"Faggot" came from the box and I felt like something swiped across the top of my head. I started to feel sick to my stomach. "Who keeps touching me on my arm?"

"Baal.... Beezle."

"Are you making me sick?"

"Yeah"

"What is in my back right pocket?"

"Bible."

The answer was correct. I often carry a small pocket Bible at negative locations. The feeling of something swiping against me happened again, this time on the side of my head. Something was taking swipes at me, and something was aware of the bible in my pocket which implied it had been watching me. A voice from the box said my name, both first and last, which further unsettled me. I tried to redirect things, asking again who the woman in the photograph was. This time there was a response of "Lea. So pretty."

"What happened to her?"

"Dead." The Mel Meter registered a drop in temperature and again, something started touching me. I demanded that nothing touch me and told it to stop immediately.

"NO." At the response a coldness surrounded me. It was as if a big freezer door had opened, and the cold was rushing out of it and onto me. Although the Mel Meter continued going off, the touching sensations stopped and the coldness slowly dissipated. I asked who was messing with the REM pod earlier. "Kid" was the response. I found that to be interesting and wondered if the spirit of the boy who had shot himself was active in the house that night.

A female voice from the box said, "visit me." Was this perhaps the succubus that had tried to attack me? I said no, I would not be visiting. "I'm going to bring a Rabbi in here, what do you think about that?"

"You'll find out." Something touched my hand; it was very solid, and I jumped a bit at the sensation. The coldness started to surround me again and "get them" came from the box. "No, you're not going to get us. Are you from the Dybbuk box or the house?"

"House."

Other random, but relevant words came out of the ghost box, including my name. I had been feeling more and more sick as the session progressed, and finally put an end to it and called it a night.

Day 17

Jerry started things off with a session by himself in the middle bedroom. He turned on the recording of the Jewish prayers, and right away there was a tapping noise coming from somewhere in the house. As he walked around the room attempting to get a response, he said it felt as if something was following him the entire time. Watching on the camera feed we could tell he was on edge. After no responses, he left the prayers going and came downstairs. As soon as he reached Bambi and me, there was a loud thump from the room he'd just left. He told us things didn't feel right in the house and Bambi and I both agreed with him. He then grabbed some holy water and headed back upstairs.

He started provoking once he was back on the upper level and I heard a loud, growling noise right away. He called out that something had scraped his back and the Mel Meter started going off. I ran upstairs and checked his back. Sure enough, there were large, red marks all up and down his back. I took the bottle of holy water and began to spray a perimeter around us. At the center of the room, I noticed a temperature drop and something swiped across my arm. We then heard a strange, mechanical noise. Looking over at the table where our equipment was sitting, we noticed a toy monkey had shifted from its original position. Its arms were now closer together than they had been. The monkey was an old battery-operated toy, a circus monkey with a pair of cymbals in its hands. What was really spooky was the toy hadn't worked the whole time we'd been at the house, and there weren't even any batteries in it. Earlier when I had tried to provoke some activity, one of the things I'd said was, "Make the monkey move."

We were hearing a wide range of unexplainable noises all around us. Again, Jerry cried out about his back, this time saying that something was pulling on his shirt. He was facing me, and I was only about two feet away from him. I moved to where I could see behind him and I could see that something, some force, was pulling on his shirt. There was nothing visible touching him, no equipment, no furniture, or anything else in the room. Both of Jerry's hands were busy holding the camera rig, and he kept saying my name over and over because the feeling was freaking him out. Whatever was causing the tug on his shirt was invisible to the human eye.

"Let's get out of here!" I yelled. I knew we had to pull back and reevaluate the situation, so we made a beeline down the stairs. I can't describe in words the fear that had overcome me as I realized something unseen had scratched Jerry on the back, and that I had seen, with my own eyes, something invisible tugging on his shirt with force.

"Holy hell, my back," Jerry said. I reached over and touched his back; it was ice cold, as cold as something straight out of the freezer. Jerry lifted his shirt, and he was covered in goosebumps. Things had been so intense that Jerry said he was done for the night.

We then heard a woman's voice talking upstairs but we couldn't make out what was being said. Bambi and I decided to go up and continue the investigation. We started on the stairs and then moved to the hell room. I was feeling dizzy but pushed on. Once in the bedroom, we heard what sounded like someone walking between us. I turned the ghost box on, and we heard a voice say, "coming for you." I asked who was coming for us, but the response was vague and sounded like, "they are coming."

I turned the recording of the Jewish prayers back on. This had caused a lot of response so far and I wanted to push things a little. "I told you I was going to play the Jewish prayers if you didn't give us answers." A flurry of activity ensued. Something started touching my head and the back of my neck. The Mel Meter started going off and we heard a woman's disembodied voice yelling out loud. The voice was captured on audio, but despite numerous reviews, we couldn't make out any of the words. This voice manifested again a few moments later and again, the words could not be distinguished. It was almost as if the prayers were causing the entity pain.

We moved into the old slave quarters. We were only in the room a few seconds when I saw a wood panel against the wall shake all by itself. I almost jumped out of my shoes! I told Bambi what had happened, then I grabbed the REM pod off the floor and sat it down by the wood panel. "Are the prayers pushing you away?" There was a quick, bright flash of blue light about three feet in front of me. "Go over and touch the REM pod or go over and knock down that panel that you just shook." Again, there was another flash of unexplained light. I started feeling dizzy and something started touching my neck. Bambi announced she wasn't feeling well either. I asked some more questions, but there was no response. I then felt like something was pinching my shoulder and the room began to feel very hot. I turned off the prayer and right away, there were three distinct, loud knocks coming from the hell room.

We quickly started over to the hell room and again, there were three knocks coming out of the room. A few seconds after we entered, we heard three metallic-sounding knocks, as if something was banging on the old radiator in the room. I asked for the sound to be repeated and received a single metallic knock. Everything went quiet. It seemed something was playing with us, some supernatural game where it moved from room to room just to keep us running. I ended the session, and we went back downstairs. My shoulder was still burning where it had been pinched and Jerry verified it was really red. Another intense night at 46 Welles Street had come to an end.

Day 18

We took another break from investigating. A lot was happening to each of us on numerous levels. I'd gone through a bitter break up and I was looking for a new place to live. My wife and I still had the house together, so the situation was awkward. When Jerry called and asked if I was up for a third round of investigation, I was quite happy to say I was. I needed a break from personal issues, even if it meant going back to the Welles house.

Jerry also told me Bambi would not be joining us this time, and she would no longer be a part of the Welles investigation. I was bothered by this and prodded him for more details, but he wouldn't really say anything else. He said his friend Paul Daniels would be joining us this time around. I knew who Paul was, but I hadn't worked with him before, so I was looking forward to seeing what he brought to the table.

It was disappointing that Bambi wasn't returning. I liked her and we remain friends to this day.

After I hung up with Jerry, I sat for a moment thinking about the Welles house and how I was still so drawn to it. I told myself it was all about the loads of evidence and the paranormal activity in the place, but it was such a negative location. I had to seriously contemplate whether it still had some kind of hold on me.

Once back at the house, the next phase of our investigation started out a bit different. Mark and Debby Constantino would be joining us live via Skype to conduct a remote EVP session from their home in Reno, Nevada. The Constantinos were well-known for their EVP work, having appeared on television shows like Ghost Adventures, and they had investigated haunted locations around the country. They had quite the reputation when it came to EVP work, so we were excited about the experiment and eager to see what they might get during the remote session.

We set things up in the old slave quarters section of the house. When Mark and Debby called in, we started telling them about the various types of activity we had experienced. They were both astounded by what we described to them. We had a couple of recorders set up, and the Constantinos had a recorder going on their end. We would do the sessions simultaneously and then compare the results. I also set up a Mel Meter and a REM pod to see if something would try to manipulate either of them during the session.

The Constantinos started the EVP session off on their end, with Debby asking the first question. "How many spirits are in this house?" On playback, there was the answer of "many."

Our eyebrows went up. It was amazing that she got a response on her first question from their home in Nevada while we were more than 2500 miles away in Pennsylvania! We played back our recorders to see if we'd caught anything, but there were no responses. I kind of chuckled. Everyone knew Mark and Debby frequently conducted EVP sessions in their own home, so I said, "Maybe they thought you were asking about your own house."

"Maybe. Let me rephrase that," Debby said. "How many spirits are in the Welles house?" Again, the recorders were rewound and checked. Mark and Debby received a very light female voice, but it was inaudible. On our recorders, we too had a female voice, and it answered "many." This meant that an EVP, coming from the Welles house, was picked up by both our recorders and the recorder being used by the Constantinos all the way across the country. Several more questions were asked, but there were no immediate answers until Debby asked, "What is causing the activity in the Welles house?"

"Demon."

The voice was clear and deep, and we all verified it was saying demon. Most of us did, that is. Paul, Jerry, Debbie, and I all confirmed we heard the word. Mark, however, kept saying he didn't hear that response. The recording was played back numerous times, and each time it was clear to all of us what the word was, but Mark continued to state he didn't hear the word demon. The two of them started going back and forth about it and we just sat there listening. Mark finally said, "We'll just have to upload it because I'm just not hearing that response."

We all thought it was kind of strange, but said okay, that would be fine with us. We didn't want it to escalate into an argument. I checked the other recorder we had running, and sure enough, the word demon was clear on it also. This was a class A EVP. Sometimes, you can be involved with an investigation and spend hours and hours without capturing anything. When a piece of evidence such as this is captured, when it's so clear and is a direct answer to your question, it's very relevant.

Mark's demeanor kind of changed at this point. He seemed a bit unnerved by the whole thing, so we dropped the issue and moved on. We continued for over an hour, but no other class A EVPs were captured. We finished up the session and thanked Mark and Debby for joining us.

We continued our investigation using a hack shack and going from room to room. Jerry announced the three of us by name, and right off the box spit out several statements including "run" and "kill them." When we asked whom we were communicating with, the response was "God."

We received indications from the ghost box that there was a portal in the basement of the house, so we headed downstairs. When Jerry opened the door, he let out an exclamation and said that he saw something moving on the steps. He started to move down the steps but said the energy was intense. He then felt something pull on his jacket, so he moved back to the top of the stairs. When he asked if something had pulled on his jacket, a response of "I pulled" came from the ghost box.

"Dave, go down there." He handed me the ghost box and I had to laugh because he was a bit freaked out. I grabbed the box and went down to the bottom of the steps. "What do you want with us?"

There was no response from the ghost box, but a loud, thunderous stomping sound came from under the stairs I was standing on. It was so startling it caused me to run back up the steps. I reached the top and started explaining what I had just heard when the box said "demonic." I repeated my earlier question of "What do you want with us?" "Your soul," came the reply.

I knew a negative presence was in the basement. I started making my way back down the steps and just as I reached the bottom, I saw a black figure run from left to right across the basement. I was really on edge. The box continued to spew negative words like "kill, your soul, demonic." When I asked who was in the basement, the reply was "many."

I heard a loud exhalation of breath right next to me, and it was captured on the camera's audio. It further unnerved me, but I continued to stay. The box then told me to run.

"No, I am not running." My senses were running on high alert and I had to fight the urge to quickly run out of the basement. I even positioned myself at the bottom of the steps in the event that I needed to make a quick exit. I continued to communicate with the entity through the ghost box. Its next statements were rather creepy.

"I'm eating."

"What are you eating?"

"Blood."

"Tell us your name."

"I did."

"Are you a demon?"

"Demonic. Get out!"

"What brought you to this house?"

"Conjured."

"Is there someone or something buried in this basement?"

"Voodoo."

Something began touching the back of my head and neck. I yelled out and reached up but couldn't feel anything there. "Who just touched me? Who just touched my neck?"

"Get out."

The hack shack then went completely quiet. It was still up and running, but despite the flurry of responses and activity moments before, it had now gone silent. I switched it off, but the heavy, negative feeling remained in the basement, and there was little to nothing in terms of responses. The box, however, did repeat my name three more times.

Day 19

My level of exhaustion was off the charts. Investigating negative locations like the Welles house often left me dehydrated, so I drank four bottles of water, downed some vitamin packets, and tried to get my energy up. It was a serious effort just to move from the couch. I said some prayers of protection and after a few more hours, the mixture of prayers, water, and vitamins helped to get me feeling halfway normal.

In spite of the slight boost, the sense of dread and heaviness still lurked in every corner of the house. We headed back to the basement where the activity had been so intense the night before. We felt there was something lurking there, waiting to attack us.

We opened with a ghost box session. There was a REM pod in place near the stairs and we had a digital recorder running. Jerry was going to play a recording of an actual exorcism as a trigger. Hearing such a recording is unsettling enough, but to hear it played in such a negative location was downright disturbing. I wanted to go outside until it was over, but I decided to stay to help document any responses.

Jerry told Paul and me to leave him alone in the basement. I was against the idea, but we went upstairs and monitored him on the DVR cameras. Jerry opened with, "I am all alone and very vulnerable down here by myself. I want to meet you face to face." Paul and I heard a loud hiss over the camera's audio. Jerry then called out for one of us to stand at the top of the steps because he felt as if he were surrounded. The REM pod, which was at least twenty feet from him, started going off and did so for approximately ten seconds. Jerry yelled out, "What the fuck is that? I just heard a wicked growling sound." This was also captured, though faint, on the camera's audio.

Jerry said there were strange light anomalies in the basement with him. He put the exorcism tape on and let it play for about ten minutes, then turned it off and turned on a ghost box and called for Paul to come down to the basement.

The area was amped full of energy and I was concerned for Paul's safety, so I headed down to the basement with him. Right away, the ghost box issued a string of negative and foul words, "demon…fuck you…stab."

Paul hadn't even asked any questions. Given the dark nature of the words, he fired back at it, calling the entity a coward. It responded with "fuck you…bastard."

Paul reported a burning feeling on his hand. The ghost box then went silent for quite a while. It said my name, then fell silent again. Paul provoked some more, calling the entity a coward again and prodding it for a response, but there was nothing. We asked some more questions, but there was still nothing, so we ended the session.

We left the basement since all the activity had stopped. Jerry decided he wanted to try some solo work upstairs, so he headed up with a recorder while Paul and I monitored the cameras at control. Jerry picked up a couple of minor responses on the digital recorder, then heavy footsteps were heard above him in the attic as well as an odd "popping" sound. He moved to the back bedroom and continued with another EVP session, then started freaking out, yelling "What the hell, what the fuck? Dave!"

I yelled up the stairs to him, asking if he was okay. "No! I'm not ok!" Paul and I rushed upstairs. Jerry kept saying he wasn't okay, and he was visibly shaken. On review, we found the camera's audio had picked up what Jerry had heard—a disembodied voice whispering to him. We all then went back downstairs to take a break and regroup.

During our research on the Welles house, we had heard stories of blood dripping from some of the walls of the home. These kinds of stories often come with negative locations, and unless you get to see if for yourself and test it, it's hard to know what to make of the accounts. We did have a way to test the report that there had been blood on the walls, though. Paul had brought some luminol kits with him. Luminol is a special chemical used primarily by CSIs (Crime Scene Investigators), and law enforcement to gather evidence at crime scenes. The chemical reacts with proteins in blood and will cause it to show up under ultraviolet light. We mixed up a spray bottle full and headed upstairs, then went into the small room where the shotgun suicide was supposed to have taken place.

We sprayed down the walls and waited a couple of minutes for the chemical to react, then turned off the lights and broke out the black light. The left wall was clear, and so was the right, but when we got to the back wall, it lit up like someone had poured blood out of a bucket all over the wall. It was unbelievable how much blood there was glowing under the black light. I will never forget that sight as long as I live.

With this success, we moved through the rest of the house, checking it with the same process. Everything else was clear until we reached the dining room. Once again, one of the walls lit up like crazy, like a river of blood had flowed over the right-side wall of the room. We were blown away by the evidence. It appeared there was some truth to the tales of blood having covered some of the walls at the Welles house.

Day 20

It was time once again to take a break from the intensity of the Welles house. I had a lot to think about during the down time. I was left with more questions than ever, and still couldn't believe the layer upon layer of bad energy, tragedy and misery that was at the home. We learned there were tales of black magic and conjuring taking place at the house over the years. One couple who had lived there believed their baby, which was still in the womb at the time, would be a demon. They were so convinced that they went to a spiritualist doctor to have him bless the unborn child. There was also a carpet in the home, put there in the 1970s, reputed to be able to confuse spirits because of its pattern.

Numerous neighbors told us the home was also connected to another family, one that experienced a very well-known negative haunting in the nearby town of Pittston, PA. Reportedly, two of the family's daughters had lived in the Welles house. The story was reported to us by so many people independently that Jerry and I, accompanied by a local reporter, located the family's home and knocked on their door. We spoke with the man at length about the Welles house. He denied ever living in the place, yet he was able to describe the house to a tee, including the back yard and the alley behind the house.

Having spent many years in law enforcement, it's in my nature to listen carefully to people's accounts. I got all kinds of red flags listening to the man speak and he contradicted himself numerous times. It's not something that would hold up in a court of law, but to me, it was a clear sign that there was more to the story. At the least, it was interesting to learn more about the case I was investigating.

Other accounts related to the house included stories of children levitating above their beds, floating across the room, and hovering above their dressers. One account that really stuck in my mind, as mentioned earlier in the account of this investigation, involved a young girl who was at the top of the main staircase. It looked as if she tripped at the top of the steps, and as she started to fall, it appeared as if something unseen caught her in midair and carried her all the way down the stairs in a slow, controlled manner into the arms of her father who was waiting at the bottom of the steps. He had witnessed the whole event and was stunned beyond belief.

We were also able to interview a couple of people who had lived in the house when they were growing up. Now middle-aged, they were able to confirm some of the accounts. They reported seeing numerous shadow figures in the home and said that it was common to hear strange voices and animal sounds, including growls and hissing noises.

The call to investigate soon came again. Jerry rang and asked if I was up for yet another round. I told him of course I was. As had become the norm, the team was changing yet again and this time it was Paul who would not be joining us. There was exciting news though. Jerry told me that JZ, a renowned investigator, would be joining us for a couple of days to give us his insight on what might be going on at the property. I was honored to have the opportunity to investigate with a man of JZ's experience and reputation, so now I was really looking forward to more time at the house, in spite of the negative baggage it carried.

I picked Jerry up at an airport in Jersey and we headed for the house. It was a three-hour drive, and it gave us time to talk about some of the things we were going to try during this phase of the investigation. We arrived at the house late that night, and by the time we made a run to the store and unloaded all our gear, we decided we would just rest for the night.

JZ arrived just before noon the next day, and after meet and greets, we went to grab some food and tell him more about our experiences at the house. A reporter from one of the local newspapers had contacted us and wanted to do a story on the house and our investigation. They were slated to come by in the early evening before our investigation started for the night. The reporter showed up with a photographer in tow and I did a walk-through of the house with them, telling them some of the history of the place as well as some of the experiences we'd had during our time there. They made notes, took a few photos and were soon on their way.

The night started off active. We were all downstairs when we heard an unexplained dragging sound coming from the second floor. We all looked at each other to confirm that everyone had heard it. We did some basic sweeps of the house, then headed up the stairwell. On the steps, hack shack in hand, Jerry asked, "Do you want us to go upstairs?"

A voice from the box responded "Please." When the guys asked the spirit to state its name, the response was, "That's a good one…fuck you, John."

More questions were asked. At one point, JZ asked again for the spirit's name. The response was, "Mark. I hate you."

When JZ asked for the Bishop's name, the box responded, "Robert."

We had to wonder if this referred to Bishop Robert McKenna. McKenna worked on many cases with Ed and Lorraine Warren. JZ probed further, asking what year the Bishop had been in the house. There was no response from the ghost box, but at this moment, the stair rail that JZ was leaning on shook. No one else was touching the rail at the time so it was clear that some unseen force had caused the movement. JZ asked, "Are you the one that died on the staircase?" "Yep," came the quick response.

JZ asked the spirit if it had been in the house a long time. There was nothing from the ghost box, but again, there was a physical response. This time, it was a loud stomping noise from upstairs. Even though the ghost box was turned up full volume, we still heard the sound that came from above us. As we started moving up the stairs, the ghost box told us to "get out."

We moved into one of the bedrooms upstairs and the box started spitting out a series of threats directed toward Jerry, saying it was going to hurt him. JZ shook his head and said, "Don't even attempt it." The room became filled with the overwhelming smell of feces. It was foul and intense and in an intelligent interaction, the voice over the box told us, "choke on it."

"Tell us your name," demanded JZ in a stern voice.

We were told to get out again, then Jerry said he was starting to feel sick. As soon as he stated this, the box said "demonic."

"Are you not human? How many of you are here?" JZ asked.

"Seven."

"Why are you here?"

"Trick."

"Are you with the land?"

"Welles…payback."

"Is that you making that smell?"

"Yes."

"Tell me the lady's name."

"Lorraine."

"Are you with the (Dybbuk) box?"

There was no answer to JZ's question about the dybbuk, but then the ghost box said my name. JZ asked Jerry who opened the box and Jerry replied, "Me." The ghost box quickly said, "Me" in a tone as if it was mocking him.

"Are you with Jerry or the box?"

"Jerry."

Jerry rushed out of the room. He was still feeling sick, and it had only intensified as the fecal smell had become almost overpowering. We all left the room to get some air, with Jerry rushing off to apparently go throw up. While we were outside taking a break, JZ started talking about all the strange sounds the house produced. He said they were not the normal sounds of an old home. He also noted how oppressive it felt inside the house.

We resumed our investigation in the living room with a ghost box session. When Jerry switched the box on, it immediately said "devil." JZ and I looked at each other, "Here we go again," I thought, more implications of a demonic presence. It had been a constant in the house. JZ began the dialogue.

"Can you tell us your name?"

"Hurt you."

"Why do you want to hurt someone?"

"David."

Before JZ even had a chance to ask his next question, the box said my name again. "Why do you want to hurt David?"

"To make him pay. You're gonna die for it."

"Why are you gonna die for it?"

"We're gonna get you."

"Are you going to tell us your name tonight?"

"Get out! Mark."

"What about Mark?"

"The one."

We all commented on how drained we felt. It was as if something was sucking out all our energy during each session. The box interrupted us and told us to "wait."

"Wait for what?" asked Jerry.

"The devil."

"What am I waiting for?"

"Satan."

"Is this land sacred to you?"

"Of course?"

"Who brought the bones in?"

"Coven…getcha!"

I was hearing strange noises coming from upstairs all during this exchange. Again, everyone in the house was accounted for and no one was on the second level. John asked, "What do you want to see happen in this house?"

"Die here."

A series of odd, seemingly random words then came from the box, "have them…keep them…motherfucker." It got more negative as it continued. After a brief break, the next thing said was, "pray to the Bishop."

"Why should we pray to the Bishop?"

"For forgiveness. The one."

"Bishop McKenna? Do I need to bring him back?"

"Mess with him. He's coming."

"Who is going to come here?"

"Evil."

"Who was the priest that died on the porch?"

"We got his blood. Behind you, your neck."

I wasn't aware at the time, but this would later appear to have been a warning for what would happen to me later during the investigation. Jerry continued with the ghost box interactions. He said, "I want you to throw something in the kitchen right now." Immediately, we all heard a loud thump upstairs.

"You know we will do it," the box said.

Again, there was a loud thumping sound, but this time coming directly from the kitchen.

"More?"

"Yeah, more," said Jerry. A creepy, mocking laugh squawked from the box. JZ asked the spirit once again to reveal its name. A horrible hissing sound emerged, followed by a female voice screaming out in pain. It was horrific and we decided to turn the box off and switch over to an Ovilus to see if it would get any responses. JZ and I both noted again how exhausted we were. Jerry asked how many spirits were there and the Ovilus said, "Ten."

JZ asked how many were in the coven and the Ovilus replied, "Thirteen." The device then said "walk" just as we heard something walking upstairs, followed by a dragging noise and the box saying "upstairs."

JZ asked, "Who brought you in here?"

"Mary."

We then heard footsteps coming down the main staircase to our right. The REM pod at the bottom of the steps took a couple of hits, sounding off its alarm. JZ said, "The game is up! Mary figured you out, didn't she?" A flurry of footsteps echoed from upstairs. The Ovilus began spitting out random words, and to all our surprise —the ghost box turned itself back on. The box had been sitting on a table since we finished the earlier session. The closest person was a few feet away, and not one of us had touched it. In order to turn the box on, you have to physically press down on the button that turns it off and on. JZ looked at us and said, "I can't believe the evidence you guys are getting out of this house," then continued to address the spirits. "You know I have figured it out, right?"

"What?"

"Your game."

There were countless, unexplained noises coming from upstairs. We kept hearing footsteps walking around, and the box seemingly tried to shift gears, saying, "Dave...worried...Mom."

"That's got nothing to do with what we are talking about right now," I said.

Whatever was communicating was clearly trying to get at me personally. I had lost my Mom in 1992 when she died in an accident. I was unnerved and a bit pissed off that some entity was talking about deeply personal matters. It was as if it was letting me know it was aware of intimate things about my life. There was the sound of more movement on the main staircase, and we were all on edge as the energy and power around us felt as if it continued to build. We heard a loud hissing sound and JZ said "What the hell is that?" He again made a comment about how drained he felt; we all felt drained, so it was easy to relate to his feeling.

"Carpet" the Ovilus said. It was an odd word to hear but Jerry and I had pulled up an old carpet in the house previously. We looked at each other, puzzled, and Jerry asked the box, "What about the carpet?"

"Closet." Again, it was a curious response. The only carpet we had left was in the closet upstairs in the old slave quarters. We decided to see if there was something more to this. Grabbing some tools, we headed upstairs to the closet. We tore up the remaining carpet and examined the floorboards. One of them was loose, so using my buck knife, I pried it up, revealing a hollowed-out area. It looked like something was kept there at some point in time, but not anymore. It was yet one more mystery of the house without a ready answer.

Day 21

During our initial look at the history of the Welles house, a local resident told us about a Native American medicine man who had helped one of the previous owners. We hoped to interview this man, and we pressed hard to try and meet him, but the answer was basically a very firm "No way in hell." We were told the gentleman was very powerful within the Native American community, but he refused to discuss the house or things that had happened there. We also discovered he was a well-known lobbyist in Washington, D.C., and had done extensive work on Native rights issues. This was an additional reason he didn't want any involvement with the case. We were disappointed but continued forward with our investigation. We were so engrossed with the work we had all but forgotten the Native elder and his involvement. Imagine our surprise when we suddenly received word that the medicine man had decided he needed to meet with us! Reportedly, this elder had spent a lot of time fasting and praying about the situation at the house, and the spirits had told him he needed to speak with us. He wanted to meet in person. Naturally, we were excited about the news. I couldn't help but wonder what a man of such knowledge and wisdom would be able to tell us about the house and the land.

Our contact told us he would call us back to arrange the time and location of the meeting. He emphasized the meeting was "off the record" and we shouldn't tell anyone where or when we were meeting. We all readily agreed. The call came later that day. The meeting was to take place at a small restaurant in a different part of town. I put the address in my GPS, and we set out.

We left early, not wanting anything to interfere with our meeting, and hung out in a coffee shop near the restaurant to burn some time and speculate about what we might learn. A few minutes before the appointment, we found the restaurant with an empty front lot and only two cars in the rear. We got out of the truck, a little nervous about there being no one around, and headed in through the back door of the restaurant. A very big man with a Russian accent met us at the door and directed us into a separate dining room where we saw two men sitting in the far corner, our contact and the medicine man. One by one, we introduced ourselves. First JZ, then Jerry, and then me. When JZ shook the man's hand, he glanced over to us with a look of surprise on his face. I thought this was strange but said nothing. When I shook the man's hand myself, I understood JZ's reaction. I can only describe what I felt as a wave of energy coming off of him. I'd never felt anything like it in my life. It was as if you could feel his power or spirit. It was super strong, and I knew I was in the presence of a very good man.

He invited us to sit down and began to tell us about himself. He talked about his people, explained who he was and told us about his grandmother. She had been a powerful medicine woman for the tribe and the legacy was passed down to him. Now, he was the leader of his people. He showed us many old personal photos of family and his tribe, as well as photos of the land and valley the Welles house was built on.

There were disturbing pictures too. They showed desecrated

Native American graves on portions of the valley floor. Many of these were on the very spot where the house was built. This proved the story that the Welles house was built on top of sacred Native burial grounds and had to be a likely reason for the high levels of paranormal activity in the house. He went on to describe how numerous battles were fought between his tribe and the early white settlers that came into the area. He told us the valley was where his people grew their medicine, due to the crystal clear, natural spring water that flowed out of the mountains and ground there. It was difficult and disheartening to sit and listen to these stories, yet another example of how the Native people were thrown off lands they had occupied for thousands of years before white settlers arrived.

He eventually shifted the topic and started telling us things about the house, things that really blew our minds. He told us that water ran in the house. We all glanced at each other because we knew this to be true. The basement was made from hand-cut stone and when it rained hard, water would run into the basement. The original part of the basement was built in the late 1700s along with the first part of the house.

We asked if he'd ever been inside the house and he assured us he had not. Jerry asked him how he knew about the water running through the foundation since he'd never been in the basement. He told us the spirits had given him this information.

He said when the land was taken from his people, their graves were dug up and robbed. Sacred items were stolen from the burial sites and this unleashed what he described as guardians in the forms of spirits. These guardians were assigned to protect the sacred Native site and they had been disturbed. Jerry asked him about the family who believed their baby had become possessed while still in the womb. He confirmed the story and told of his friendship with the doctor in the case. He said there were ceremonies performed in order to cleanse the unborn child of any negative spirits that may have attached. He bluntly told us he would not go into any more detail about the situation, and we knew not to press.

He did continue with further information about the house. He said other negative spirits were brought into the home and onto the land by people that were not white. We knew he was referring to some of the slaves that had worked the plantation. Some of the slaves had been brought over from Haiti and still practiced their Native Vodoun traditions. It was yet another layer of what was affecting the Welles house, yet beyond that there was more. He told us that many years after the slaves, other people brought in more negative spirits by practicing dark forms of witchcraft. It was an amazing conversation. He was filling in gaps and confirming many of the various aspects we had only heard bits and pieces of. He told us the only reason he had chosen to meet with us was that he felt we genuinely wanted to somehow appease the spirits there, and he wanted to help us do it by providing as much information as he could.

He told us the first thing we needed to do was sage the house and cleanse it with smoke. He said to get an abalone shell, white sage, and a feather, and to go through the house in each room, pushing the smoke around the room and into each corner. He said this would quell the evil ones down but not get rid of them. He then told us the only way to make the Native American spirits happy was to have the house completely torn down, and to build a beautiful garden on the property with herbs, flowers, and some sort of water feature such as a small pond with running water. This, he said, would appease the restless Native American guardians and honor the burial grounds. In turn, the guardians would keep other negative spirits away from the area.

It was a wonderful idea, but unfortunately it wasn't something that was within our power to accomplish. We thanked him for taking the time to meet with us and said our goodbyes, and he sent us away with a blessing. I walked out of the meeting stunned and quiet. I felt honored at having met the man, and it had been an amazing experience to sit in the presence of someone with such power and spiritual energy about them.

To this day, JZ and I still occasionally talk about the power the Native man had and how special it was to have met him. We knew the man had brought us there in hopes that we could help the restless spirits on the land and bring some peace to his ancestors. I still wish I could have done more.

Back at the house, JZ and I were still talking about the meeting with the medicine man. We were a bit apprehensive about doing another round of investigation, since we weren't sure if there would be any backlash from the entities in the home knowing we'd met with a shaman. Nevertheless, we got back to work. I placed a REM pod midway up the stairway and we gathered in the living room. JZ made a comment about how surprised he was that Jerry and I had any energy left at all. It was apparent he was very drained himself. We turned on the Ovilus and Jerry asked if anyone was still there with us.

Right away, the device said JZ's name. When JZ responded asking what it wanted, we heard the sound of footsteps upstairs. A string of words then came from the Ovilus: jewelry, share, crash.

"What did you say?" JZ asked, snapping to attention.

Jerry repeated the words that had been said and JZ got really perturbed. "Stop playing fucking head games," JZ said.

It was clear that the words were related to something very private for JZ. Yet again, whatever the entity in the house was, it enjoyed showing that it knew personal information about each of us, things only the individual could know.

There was more movement upstairs and we could feel the house becoming more active by the moment. Jerry tried running a hack shack at the same time we had the Ovilus going. We heard a string of things from the devices, "I want you dead. Demon, very powerful." We also started hearing another language coming from the box. Although it sounded like a Native American dialect, we were unable to confirm what it was. Was this perhaps because we had met with the shaman earlier in the day?

Another response came across the box, saying, "had a heart attack." Was this the spirit of the man who had reportedly dropped dead on the porch of the home from a sudden heart attack? Perhaps his spirit was still stuck at the house.

Jerry said he needed to take a break, so JZ and I started up a ghost box in the living room. I opened the session stating my name and JZ's. I asked for the spirits that had been trying to communicate with us upstairs to come and talk. The box replied, "talk."

"Yes, talk."

"What for? Down."

"Yeah, come down here. What's your name?"

"Tony."

"Is your name Mark? Yes, or no."

"That's right."

The voice was deep and rough and JZ asked, "What's your real name?"

"Salty."

"You're a smart-ass. What's your real name?" There was no response for a few moments, so JZ tried a different question: "Do you know any of our names?" A voice from the box immediately stated both of our names, then followed with "get out, don't like questions."

"Where in the house are you right now?" we asked.

"Behind you." The hair on the back of my neck and arms went up and I had goose bumps all over my body. Something was very close to me.

"Get out...get out...get out" the box kept saying. Clearly something was trying to push us out. We ignored it and I asked another question, "Who do you worship?"

"Ancient."

"How many of you are in this house?"

"Holy trinity."

"What do you think about the Father, Son and the Holy Spirit?"

"Mark five." It was yet another reference to the biblical passage about demons. JZ then asked, "In 1972, who was here?"

"Preacher."

"In 1972, who was here?"

"Warren." JZ shifted in his seat and asked the question a third time, "In 1972, who was here?"

"Ed."

Ed Warren, the renowned ghost hunter, was also a member of the clergy. We knew he and his wife Lorraine had visited the house, but there was never any confirmation they'd been there in 1972. According to a news article, they had stopped by the home in 1980, but there was no record of them conducting an investigation in the house.

There was a loud thumping sound, like a body had fallen down the stairs. Jerry was in our line of sight, sitting at his computer. The box said our names again. We had a candle burning on the table in front of us, and I said, "Come over here and blow the candle out." Three seconds later the flame on the candle started to flicker wildly as if something was attempting to blow it out. JZ asked "Who is going through the room?"

"Demon." Out of nowhere, the temperature in the room dropped drastically. I looked at JZ and said, "There's something in this room, it's cold as shit in here." The box replied, "Yeah."

"How many are in this room right now?" JZ asked.

"Count 'em."

"You count em."

There was no further response to the question, so I chimed in, "Tell us the name of the priest that visited this house."

"Ed…Warren. Ed's gone."

"Tell us the name of the woman who last lived in this house."

"I knew her. Killed. Coming."

"Who's coming?"

"Incuba."

"What is your sole purpose in this house?"

"Death and arrival."

"Do you want us to burn the house down?"

"God, I hope. Friend." We interpreted this to be a trapped spirit, hoping we would destroy the house and somehow set it free. There continued to be a range of strange sounds coming from upstairs, including footsteps and loud thumping sounds. "Come down here and talk to us."

"Take a Bible."

"Tell us your name."

"You know me." I turned the ghost box off. I wanted to continue the session but JZ needed a break. The whole time we'd been conducting the session in the living room, the REM pod on the second floor in the hell room had been taking hits. Between that and all the anomalous sounds, I wanted to go up and see what kind of evidence I could gather.

Upstairs, I decided to take a stern stance with the session. I stated loudly, "I want to know the name of the evil female spirit that is in this house." The REM pod went off with a flurry, lighting up like a Christmas tree. A voice out of the SB-7 I was holding responded with "Beezle."

"WHAT IS YOUR NAME? Is there a succubus in this room? I wanna know who is in this room with me right now. Tell me your name!"

"Ba'al"

"Confirm that, is that your name, yes, or no?"

"Demon."

During this entire exchange, the REM pod was going crazy, taking hit after hit. I was unnerved at the information; a known demonic name had been stated. There were continued loud bumps and bangs coming from the room I was standing in. I decided to see if the entity was intelligent by asking, "What is in my right front pocket right now?" I pulled the item out of my pocket and held it up. "This is it, what am I holding?"

"A knife." It was the correct answer. The energy in the room was at a fever pitch, and I knew I was dealing with something very dark that could see me and knew who I was. The phrases coming out of the SB-7 began to turn more negative.

"Watch out."

"What do I need to watch out for?"

"Him."

"Talk to me."

"I did, and a demon."

"Are you an old evil or an ancient one?"

"I'm evil."

"What names do you go by?"

"Us."

"How many names do you go by?"

"Many."

"Was there witchcraft practiced in this house?"

"Yeah."

"Tell me the family name of the people who practiced witchcraft in this house."

"Fuck you."

"Did you make sure that JZ would come to this house to investigate with us?"

"Call him. We want him. We'll get him."

"So, you meant for JZ to come here with us?"

"Yes!" I was startled by something touching my back. I began to hear weird snarls and growling sounds coming from the box. "I'm only going to be here a few more minutes. If there is anything you want to tell me, now is the time."

"You're dead."

"What, you are threatening me by saying I'm dead?"

"Kill."

"I'm not dead, you're dead." There was a change in what was coming over the box. There were two different voices, and it sounded like a pair of spirits having a discussion with each other:

"You want me to do it?"

"No, I'll do it."

It was as if they were discussing which one of them was going to attempt to hurt me. I again felt as though something was all around me. There was a strong feeling of static electricity in the air, especially around my arms and the back of my neck. "Are you doing that to me?"

"Yeah."

"Back off."

"Get out!"

"I am not getting out."

"I warn you."

"What are you warning me of?"

"Demon." More snarling and growling came from the box. I started to feel like something was choking me and I began to cough uncontrollably. "All right, that's it!" I said, I reached over to turn the box off and the voice said, "Put your face down."

I had been choked by an unseen force. I was still coughing wildly as I headed out of the room. I was shaken, being both verbally and physically attacked, and I moved quickly back down the stairs, fighting to stay conscious. The coughing was still out of control and JZ and Jerry rushed over to see if I was all right. I could barely talk as I headed out the door, trying to get my breath back. The guys were right behind me, asking me what happened. "Something got me," I managed to say. It took me almost ten minutes before I regained my composure and overcame what happened.

We decided it was time to stop the investigation since things had reached another level of danger. JZ was completely exhausted, and he would be leaving the next morning. I had to take Jerry back to the airport, so it would be a long day for all of us. Truthfully, I was ready to call it quits, jump in my truck, and head home right that instant. But I knew Jerry needed a ride back to catch his flight the next day, and I didn't want to leave him and JZ alone in the house the rest of the night after all that had happened.

I stayed outside for a while. In fact, it took me a long time that night to get my nerve back up to even head back inside the house. I finally managed to walk back through the door. I packed up my gear, all the while saying protective prayers. I tried to get some sleep, but I couldn't. I lay there all night, thinking about the hell room above us and what was in there. I thought about the warning I had received earlier in the investigation. Something in the Welles house wanted me dead, it had threatened me, then followed through and made an attempt. The final hours of the night passed very slowly.

Day 22

We were up early. I hadn't slept anyway, and I just wanted out of the house. I helped JZ load his gear into his car, we said our goodbyes, and he was on his way back home. Jerry and I got some caffeine, finished packing and loading our own gear, then hit the road. I soon felt much lighter and relieved. As always, leaving the Welles house felt like a heavy weight dropped away. I told Jerry I was certain I'd never go back to the place. I was done with all the evil there.

But the house wasn't quite done with me.

An hour and a half into our three-hour drive, we ran into a massive traffic jam. It was very odd as the traffic was at a complete standstill on both sides of the interstate. Initially we thought it was road construction, so we just sat there talking about all the crazy things we had experienced during our investigation at the house. But the minutes ticked by and soon we had been sitting for forty-five minutes and barely moved.

We started getting concerned about Jerry missing his flight, so using our phones we started searching for road information. Soon enough we found out there had been a massive accident and officials were calling for delays of more than three hours. There was no way to get around it and we knew Jerry would definitely miss his flight home. He got on the phone with the airline and explained what was going on, asking if he could get on a later flight that night. After an hour of conversation, he found out the only flight he could get was the following day. I was still searching for a way to get off the road and go a different route, but now that Jerry was stuck until the next day, we had to decide what to do.

"We might as well go back to the Welles house for one more investigation," Jerry said.

I was dead set against it, but I knew we were both tight on money and really had no other choice but to sleep at the house that night. I truly felt the house and the entities within it had something to do with the whole thing.

It fit perfectly with my beliefs about the house, its way of calling you and trying to hold you and manipulate you. It was a place you hated to be when you were there, but you couldn't get out of your mind when you were away. I hated the place but was oddly compelled by it, and now I was on my way back there yet again.

On our way back a call came in from JZ and we put him on speaker phone. He was really upset and said, "You won't believe what happened to me." He said that as he was driving back home, his hat was suddenly knocked off his head so hard it flew into the back seat of his car. At the same time, it became difficult to steer. He was scared so bad he pulled off on the side of the road and did some cleansing. Needless to say, we were a bit taken aback by the whole thing. We told him what was going on with us, about the standstill traffic, the missed flight, and the fact we were headed back to the house for another night. He was adamantly against us going back, but we explained to him that we really didn't have any other choice in the matter.

He told us there was no way he would return to the Welles house. We talked with JZ a while longer, then hung up. We were now even more concerned about having to return to the house. We decided to stop and get some food, mainly so we could kill some more time and spend less of it in the Welles house.

It was five in the evening by the time we arrived. Pulling up in front of the place, I felt a knot in my stomach. I couldn't believe I was back. We took a small amount of gear in, just a few simple essentials for the investigation. We soon had a fire going in the wood stove and our gear out and loaded with fresh batteries.

There were already strange sounds coming from all over the house. We were still getting ready, and Jerry was in the bathroom when the ghost box inside of his bag turned on all by itself. The sound startled me and as I was trying to take it in, a flashlight in my gear case also turned on by itself. I was really starting to get unnerved. This wasn't the first time equipment had behaved strangely in the house, and we'd had numerous incidents of devices coming on by themselves, but it was another sign the energy in the house was quickly ramping back up, and after being pulled back to the place by such a weird set of circumstances, it was just disturbing.

We did a brief session on the stairway, with Jerry challenging the spirits to push him down the steps. There was a loud bang from the suicide room upstairs, then Jerry said he felt dizzy. There were more noises from upstairs and we decided to head up. Jerry kept saying he didn't feel right, and when I looked at him, something seemed very off.

The atmosphere in the house felt truly evil. Jerry looked at me and said, "What? What?"

I hadn't said anything, but he thought he had heard me speak. He then yelled out, "Whoever is responsible for all the pain, sadness, and oppression in this house, show yourself."

Before he even finished speaking, we both saw a shadowy figure in the doorway of the back bedroom. Jerry yelled again for the entity to show itself, and the Mel Meter took a hit, registering a temperature drop.

Jerry ran downstairs and quickly came back up with a bottle of holy water. He began spraying it all around the room which had begun to get increasingly active. The Mel Meter was going nuts and there were continued bangs and thumps all around us. He continued spraying the holy water, hoping to provoke even more reactions. We turned on the Ovilus and it stated "man."

"Will you ever show yourself?"

"Mirror." We'd brought a scrying mirror in with us and thought perhaps this was what it was referring to. Jerry went to grab a candle and I said, "Tell me what you are going to show us in the mirror."

"Them."

"Who is them?"

"Hair."

Jerry yelled up saying he couldn't find a candle and told me to just keep doing a session alone for a few minutes.

"Alone."

"Yes, I'm alone." The weird noises continued all around me and from the back room.

"How many of you are here with us now?"

"Karen and eight."

Jerry finally returned. He lit the candle and we set it by the scrying mirror. He called out to the spirits to reveal themselves in the mirror. After just a few seconds, Jerry said he didn't like what was going on and that he felt really weird. He said his face was changing in the mirror and he asked out loud if something was coming through. He kept saying he didn't like what was going on, then started mumbling incoherently to himself. All at once he jumped completely back in the chair. It was so dramatic that it made me jump too, and I asked him what was wrong. He started rubbing his eyes and I asked him again if he was all right. He said no, jumped up out of the seat and said he had to get out. I followed him down the steps and as we were leaving, the Ovilus back in the room said my name. Without any clear purpose, Jerry went all the way through the house and started walking down into the basement. I asked him loudly why, and it was as if he snapped out of a trance. "I don't know. I thought you were down there."

"Let's take a break and go outside."

When we got outside Jerry explained what he was experiencing during the scrying session. He described how he saw his face changing and melting into another form.

We stayed outside for almost half an hour clearing our heads. Once back inside, we headed back up to use the mirror and a ghost box to see if we could communicate with whatever had affected Jerry. He started the session with, "Are you from this house?" The camera I was running went out of focus, and there was a bright light anomaly over the top of Jerry's head. From the ghost box, we could hear weird growls and screams. "What is it about the number seven?"

"I'm your God."

"You're not my God."

The next response came from the Ovilus, which we'd forgotten was still running.

"Beezlebub." There was a string of words out of the device followed by "go…to…cellar…alone." This alarmed both of us, especially since Jerry had just tried to make a solo trek down there. "Tell me who is your master?"

"The devil."

"Are you the lord of the flies?"

"Abacus."

"Who is Abacus?" There was no response, but a quick search on a Demonology site revealed that Abacus was a demonic name associated with the Ouija board. As soon as we made the discovery, the box spoke as if in confirmation.

"I'm a demon. The devil."

I was covered in cold chills and I was ready to get the hell out of the house. There were a loud series of thumps out of the box along with a growling voice we couldn't understand clearly.

We were both drained and freaked out by the activity and responses, so we shut all the equipment off and packed up. There was a long day of driving ahead but I found it impossible to get any decent rest. I spent a restless night fighting off images of demonic entities and listening to the weird sounds produced by the home.

As the hours wore on, I lay awake telling myself, yet again, that it would be the last time I stepped foot in the evil Welles house. This time, I hoped that it was true.

The Investigative Journal of Dave Spinks

Testimonials

Bambi

A Statement on my Personal Experience at the Welles House

"I've always prided myself on being open to talk about nearly everything. I have to admit, writing this piece about my time in the Welles house proved to be really difficult. In fact, I didn't talk about it for the longest time because of what I experienced inside the house, and also how it affected me outside of the house.

"I had always been drawn in by the paranormal after living in a haunted house. I was also a loyal fan of paranormal television shows and videos online. Before this investigation, I had very little experience.

"Then I was invited to investigate the Welles house. I wanted to experience a haunted location, with real and respected investigators. To say the least, be careful what you ask for. I'm not going to go into every detail of what happened during the time I spent in the Welles house, but I can say it's not something I enjoy revisiting in my memory.

"When I first arrived, I was anxious but overall excited, but that seemed to fade when I actually entered the house. It felt heavy. Almost like I was constantly walking down a narrow hallway, no matter where I went. I had this strange sense of being uncomfortable, yet not wanting to leave at the same time.

"Personally, I feel like I made many mistakes while I was there. What people fail to understand is, sure—there are times where you don't encounter anything, disprove claims, or even disprove any paranormal activity at all; but there is that possibility of messing with something that isn't in your control, or messing with something that you cannot begin to understand.

"Up until now, I regretted going to that house. I would constantly think 'was it worth it? Look how much has changed since then,' and there was, and still is a sort of existential dread I associate with it.

"I'm glad I met Dave, he was a mentor and a father figure while I was there. His biggest stance that I noticed was that he wouldn't touch the Ouija board. No matter how many times he was asked to, he had nothing to do with it.

"I, however, was foolish enough to accompany other investigators on the other side of the board during our time there. Most of the time I was just focused on my energy on the meters around me and making sense of what the board was spelling.

"Then it took a turn.

"It wasn't about the house anymore, who had lived there or died there, or if a spirit was present. While I was focused elsewhere, something decided to focus on me, personally.

"I began to spell out what I thought was an answer to a question, but it was an unrelated answer. The board had spelled out '4 dead children.' I felt it. I felt an indescribable amount of dread. I felt it was a personal attack. I called out and asked 'whose?'

"The planchette immediately spelled out 'yours.' I was instantly freaked out. Years previous to the investigation I had suffered through 2 miscarriages. I hadn't told anyone about that, and there was no way they could have known.

"When I left the house, I suffered another miscarriage, and then a short time later, I found out I was pregnant again.

"During the entire pregnancy I was plagued with thinking he wasn't going to make it. I would flashback to the Ouija board and being in that house. I refused to look at infant clothing or even prepare myself for having a living child. I already knew the answer. I already felt the dread. Not only because of the Ouija board, but because of what had happened so far as well.

"When he was born, he wasn't breathing, I didn't get to hold him for nearly 2 hours while I was healing, and he was healing. It took 2 days after him being born to realize he was okay. He is almost 2 years old now, and every so often my mind wanders to that specific memory. Of sitting across the Ouija board and watching it spell out those letters. He is technically my 4th child. I cannot stress enough how these things can affect you for the rest of your life. Do I think the house caused what happened? Obviously not, but in that moment, during that investigation, I feel like I channeled someone or something that knew."

Norene

How in the Hell Can You Stay in That House?

"Before Halloween of 2013, I was working on a project to find a real haunted house. After searching for days, I came across information about a haunted location in Wilkes-Barre, PA. Numerous stories described the house as the area's own version of the 'Amityville Horror.'

"One article in particular really grabbed my attention. It was from a neighbor who designed an advertisement on the web hoping to help the family sell the house. The owner, Katherine Watkins, had died in the house the previous year. The article contained phrases such as 'The effect on people who lived in this house was very, very negative.' The piece also described suicides, voodoo rituals, ghost sightings, and other unexplained phenomena. The advertisement, which was listed in the *Wilkes-Barre Independent Gazette*, led to two showings of the property, both to ghost hunters. 'They were interested because it was haunted,' the story said.

"The 2,092-square-foot home was assessed at $63,200 and listed for sale at $30,000, though the neighbor said the family would consider any fair offers. Potential buyers could contact her at the number listed on the site. I tried calling the number, but it was no longer an active listing. I assumed the number was disconnected because of the interest in paranormal groups wanting to attain access to the property after all its publicity.

"I then started looking for an **active** real estate listing for 46 S. Welles St., Wilkes-Barre, Pa. I found the listing of the house on my searches under haunted houses. The listing was with a local real estate agent. When I called the agent and asked him about the property, he was unenthusiastic about the phone call. He proceeded to tell me that he indeed had the listing, but that was about it, he had nothing to do with the house. I thought to myself, how odd is that...I was a former real estate agent, and such behavior is at the least very unusual. The agent told me I would have to call the daughter, Stacy, the current owner of the house and he gave me her phone number. I called her right away. In fact, I still have her phone number to this day. The phone directed me to an answering machine, and I left a message. Stacy called me back and I explained to her I had someone interested in her house, but this person wanted to rent for about a week or so in order for evidence to be gathered to verify the haunting.

"I talked to Stacy on a number of occasions. She and her husband Matt were trying to sell the home. It had belonged to her mother. They were both afraid its long-standing reputation as a haunted house might hinder the sale. The house was documented as being haunted long before her mother bought it in 1980 for a cheap price. Stacy was gracious enough to let the investigation move forward. During this time, Dave Spinks was one of the main investigators, spending over thirty days living in and investigating the property. I can say without hesitation that the Welles house is the site of some truly bizarre and frightening events.

"I was asked numerous times to come to the Welles house for a meet and greet event with paranormal guests. I repeatedly stated that the house gave me the creeps and that I wanted no part of the place. I refused to step foot in it. After hearing about some of the things taking place in the house, I asked some of the people investigating, 'How in the hell can you stay in that house?'

"Eventually the home was bought by an investigator, but before long he was ready to sell it. He asked me to help him find a real estate agent to list the house for sale. My search for an agent took days. I would leave messages and get no response. Sometimes I was lucky enough to actually talk to an agent on the phone, but as soon as they found out the address, they wanted nothing to do with the listing.

Some even told me their broker wouldn't even allow the listing in their office.

Norene Balovich is the host of the popular show Paranormal Zone TV.

An Unsettled Valley
David Weatherly

"You are more likely to die by homicide in Wilkes-Barre than in major cities like New York, Philadelphia, Pittsburgh, or Chicago."

This was according to a report in the *Times-Leader* of October 19, 2013. The report went on to state:

"There were 11 slayings in this city of 41,000 people this year through Friday, ranging from a bruised and battered 2-month-old boy to a 46-year-old woman allegedly shot to death by her estranged husband."

Such disturbing statistics made the homicide rate in the small area of Wilkes-Barre eight times greater than New York City for the year. As the area's crime watch coordinator, Charlotte Raup, stated: "Oh my God, we're only seven square miles."

To put the comparison further into context, New York City is 305 square miles and has a population of 8,550,405. It begs the question, what exactly is it about Wilkes-Barre that makes it so dangerous and so unsettled?

A Foundation of Conflict

Wilkes-Barre lies in the northeastern quadrant of Pennsylvania. Founded in 1769, the city is the county seat of Luzerne county and is the second largest city in the county behind nearby Scranton. Along with Scranton and Hazleton, Wilkes-Barre forms the fourth largest metro area in the state.

The city is in the center of a crescent shaped depression called the Wyoming Valley. This rich, fertile region is framed by the Pocono Mountains to the east, the Endless Mountains to the west and the Lehigh Valley to the south. The Susquehanna River flows through the center of the valley and is the northwestern border of the city.

Like the rest of the United States, the region was originally occupied by Native American tribes. For many years, the Wyoming Valley was home to the Shawnee and Delaware peoples, who used the valley as a hunting ground and as a place to gather medicinal herbs and edible plants.

The first Europeans to reach the area were a group led by John Durkee in 1769. They formed a settlement named after two members of British Parliament who were supporters of colonial America, John Wilkes, and Isaac Barre. From the very start, the area seemed prone to trouble.

As with much of the country there was conflict between the settlers and the natives. Originally, the land was occupied by an Iroquoian speaking tribe, but by the 1740s, they had been pushed out by various groups of Shawnees, Lenape, and Mahicans, who in turn had been pushed out of their territory by the Iroquois Confederacy. Conflict during the French and Indian War lead to further changes in the valley.

One large group of early settlers came from Connecticut, which had staked its own claim on the land. Armed Pennsylvanians made attempts to force the Connecticut settlers out and the conflict escalated, becoming known as the Yankee-Pennamite Wars.

The two factions put their differences aside for a time, distracted by the American Revolution and the resulting widespread conflict it brought. After the war, the two states finally came to a peaceful resolution of the dispute, with Connecticut giving up its claims to the land. The settlement remained and the citizens who stayed transferred their allegiance to Pennsylvania. Eventually, all the native land was taken as settlements grew and more people migrated to the valley.

During the War for Independence, a force of British and Tories led by John Butler raided the area. On July 3, 1778, the British force, along with 700 Indian allies, attacked and killed almost 300 people in the Wyoming Valley. The Battle of Wyoming became known as a massacre, and today a monument marks the gravesite of the victims lost in the conflict.

By the 19th century, Wilkes-Barre was a booming town. The discovery of anthracite coal in the region led to an influx of settlers, all seeking work and a better life. The ethnic mix was diverse with the highest percentage of settlers being Italian, followed closely by Polish, Irish, and then German, English and Welsh.

Fueled by the coal industry, the Wyoming Valley itself made tremendous contributions to the industrial revolution in the United States and the area became an economic and industrial powerhouse, for a time. But along with the growth there was tragedy.

A massive explosion at the Baltimore Colliery in 1919 caused the death of ninety-two miners. 1959 brought another mining calamity, the Knox Mine Disaster, the flooding of numerous mines that marked the end of coal's highpoint in the region. Just as extensive mining had created a boom, the loss of the industry caused a rapid decline.

The city suffered yet another bout of extensive flooding in 1972 when Hurricane Agnes struck. The resulting damage from the storm was another major blow to the economic health of the city. The massive storm caused the Susquehanna River to rise to a height of 41 feet, a full four feet over the limit of the city's levees. Downtown Wilkes-Barre was flooded with nine feet of water and 128 deaths were attributed to the hurricane, most of them drowning deaths from people trapped in cars. Around 400,000 homes and businesses were destroyed. Damages from Agnes in Pennsylvania reached a staggering 2.1 billion dollars.

A new water level record was set in 2011 when Hurricane Irene caused the Susquehanna River to rise again, this time to a height of 42.66 feet. The rebuilt, 41-foot levees held and protected the city from any major damage.

Various politicians and community groups have fought against the city's long decline over the years. The early 2000s saw a major push to revitalize Wilkes-Barre, but it was met with mixed reviews. The numbers remain telling.

The population has been in almost constant decline since the 1930s. Presently, the total is less than half of what it was in 1940.

In 2009, the coal city saw 31.9 percent of its population living below the poverty level, nearly double that of the state average of 16.4 percent.

In 2019, the median income for the city was $38,255, a figure 65.9% lower than the rest of the state. Going into 2021, the city's unemployment is around 13 percent.

Dark Whispers

These are certainly all elements to be considered in the health of a city and the mindset of its people, but there are other factors too. People living in the area have a high level of vitamin D deficiency, due in large part to the low levels of sunshine the valley receives, a total of only seventy days per year. Health care workers in the region report a large number of cases of SAD, or Seasonal Affective Disorder. As a result, many people are on anti-depressants. Residents also report that both air and water quality in the region are poor, leading to further health related issues.

One national poll listed Wilkes-Barre in the top five places of the largest number of unhappy people in the United States. Polls can be skewed, so they represent a fleeting opinion, but there's no getting around the number of people who make comments about the dark and depressing nature of the city.

Take this sampling of statements from area residents:

"This place is so, so gloomy. It seems like it's in a cloud of despair and the gloom and cold is hell on health and emotions. We were told it wasn't very expensive to live here, but the heating bills are hell, the water stinks, and it's hard to find work." Sara S.

"This is a small area, and you would think it would be safe, but it's not. I don't feel safe even being outside around our house. And there's a ton of sick, sick crime here. Perverts, pedophiles, you name it. We were here a month and I saw a creeper peeping in my window one night. I can't wait to leave." Angela R.

Sara and Angela are only two voices in a long list of people who are discontent with the city. Countless people interviewed had similar complaints. The themes are consistent: poor health, depression, broken marriages, high crime, and rampant drug use.

There may be other dark factors that cause the heavy feelings many people experience in the city. According to many locals, Wilkes-Barre has a high number of devil worshipers. Countless residents claim rumors of Satanism and witchcraft abound and have for years. Official reports are sketchy, yet some accounts do crop up.

In 2004, police investigated a scene in a wooded area in town that was a purported site of Satanic worship and ritual. What they found was disturbing evidence of animal mutilation and possible black magic activity. Police described a "circular-type altar" with somewhere between 25 to 30 burned and mutilated animal remains. Little information could be derived from the site and no arrests were made in connection to it; however, a year later there was another strange twist.

In the same area of the animal mutilations, a 24-year-old man was found pinned under a vehicle parked in the woods. Again, rumors of Satanic activity ran rampant but again, no solid evidence was uncovered. To many, this merely reinforced the idea there were hordes of devil worshipers in the area, and that some were active in covering up any crimes committed by Satanic covens.

It may all sound like a conspiracy theory or sick fantasy, but there's no denying that there are groups of Satanists in the area. So many it seems, that Wilkes-Barre even has its own online Satanist dating site, the Devil Dating Community of Wilkes-Barre. (As of publication, it appears this website is no longer active).

New residents in the area often quickly learn about the Satanic rumors, sometimes via direct experience with members of the dark community. Take James for instance.

"When I first moved here, this attractive girl was flirting with me, but the more I talked to her, the stranger she got. Then I found out that she was a Satanist and she told me they had a big group in the area. It freaked me out. She said there were a lot of witches into black magic and that there were spots in the woods where animal sacrifice and rituals were done; she wanted me to come along, but I said no way." James M.

James isn't alone in his experience. Another young woman reported similar encounters upon moving to the city. Julia reports that she and a girlfriend spotted a group of people in black, hooded robes coming out of the woods one night.

"We were driving back from a movie, just riding around and talking really, when the headlights caught a group of about five people pop out of the woods. They were wearing black robes with hoods over them so you couldn't see their faces. One of them was wearing a shiny, upside down pentagram. We were freaked out that they would see who we were, and we got out of there as quick as we could. We called the police, but they didn't seem too interested in the report." Julia S.

Pennsylvania itself has a long history of rich lore involving witches, witchcraft, and magic. From early settlers who brought over their European magical beliefs, to the Pennsylvania Dutch and their hex traditions, to later additions such as African Americans and their voodoo and hoodoo. The so-called "Satanic panic" of the 1980s added more fuel to the idea of rampant devil worshipers, and when modern groups like wiccans were added to the mix, it made for a curious melting pot, to say the least.

One area legend of a witch can be found in Luzerne County's Shupp Cemetery. According to local lore, the graveyard contains the tombstone of a woman named Mary, known as the "Larksville Witch." Locals report that anyone who visits the cemetery and reads the words written on Mary's tombstone will suffer a plague of terrible events. The cemetery is purported to be a site of strange, paranormal activity and Mary's legend is so well known the graveyard has been given the nickname "The Witch's Cemetery."

A few people have claimed the Luzerne County courthouse is haunted by the specter of a witch, but this seems to be a more recent idea. The courthouse does indeed have an old ghostly legend, a woman in white who haunts the second floor of the building and has been known to give government employees a fright.

There are also stories of various "witch's houses" that are to be found on the outskirts of the city. These buildings are usually long abandoned homes that have developed a reputation for being gathering places of witches and Satanists. This may be simple urban legend, but at the least, it helps perpetuate the constant stories of dark doings in and around Wilkes-Barre.

Other residents believe the heavy energy over the region is the result of a native American curse, placed on the land itself by a tribal shaman long ago, angry, and distraught over the displacement of his people.

Countless interviews with unhappy residents produce the same, or similar key words and phrases used to describe the city. "Uneasy, low vibration, cursed, disturbed, and spiritually heavy." Residents complain about long periods of bad luck, set off by moving to the city. Oddly, there are also numerous people who claim they developed unexplainable fears after moving to Wilkes-Barre.

"I was never afraid of the dark in my life. When I was a kid, I'd spend a lot of time outside at night and I loved it. I'm just over thirty years old now, and since I moved here, I'm just too frightened to go outside after dark. I can't explain it, but I know it has something to do with this place." Mark M.

The paranormal seems to come alive for some who move to the city. Take Robert who claims he was a skeptic his whole life, until he relocated to the Pennsylvania town.

"I never, ever believed in anything related to the paranormal. Not until I moved here. This place screwed me up. I've seen weird crap here. I wasn't drunk or high; I saw a black mass that moved toward us and I swear there was some kind of face in it. Then we found out our next-door neighbors were into devil worship. We moved to a different part of town, but it's not much better here. I just want to leave." Robert J.

A history of conflict, a depressing climate, high crime, rampant Satanism, and numerous claims of paranormal activity. It sounds like a disturbing mix and we can only guess at the validity of some of the factors and how they might affect the whole. Does such a dark climate make the city a haven for sinister spirits? It must be considered a possibility. As one local man noted:

"There's something terribly, terribly wrong with this place at its core. That's all there is to it. People stay sick all the time, more than should be average. There have been a lot of strange deaths around the river (the Susquehanna). Most of all, the thing I notice is when I leave there's a big, big difference in how I feel. It's like a huge weight comes off of me and the further from here I drive, the lighter I feel. But something keeps pulling me back here, and I haven't been able to get the place out of my blood yet. I wish I could leave for good, but for now, something won't let me." Alex M.

In the early morning hours of Wednesday, June 27, 2018, police were called to the Welles house to investigate a reported break-in at the property. A witness had seen someone prying the plywood off the home's back door and entering the property.

Arriving on the scene, police officers found 33-year-old Anthony Parker of Wilkes Barre inside. When officers questioned Parker about his presence in the house, he told them he was there hunting ghosts. According to the authorities, Parker was armed not with ghost hunting equipment, but with an assortment of items that included bladed brass knuckles, a pocketknife, a Bible, and a 24-inch sword strapped across his back. Parker was also carrying a Crown Royal bag filled with shotgun shells. During a search of the scene, police officers found a pistol-gripped shotgun hidden behind the house.

Parker was charged with defiant trespassing, possession of instruments of crime, weapons possession, and nighttime prowling.

To this day, rumors continue to swirl around the infamous house on Welles Street. For a time, it was reported that the city was going to have it torn down. People still trespass on the property, looking for the ghost reputed to haunt it, or just a cheap and daring thrill.

Some people claim various degrees of criminal activity take place in the home, while others claim Satanic rituals are performed inside.

Whatever the case, the house sits like a dark tomb, waiting, perhaps, for its next victims.

An Unsettled Valley

Aftermath
Dave Spinks

The Welles house investigation proved to be a gold mine of paranormal evidence compared to any of my previous experiences. There were an untold number of physical interactions between something unseen and the investigators involved, including a shirt being tugged on, hair being pulled and played with, unexplained touches, and several inexplicable scratches on one investigator. There was also a tangible heaviness felt by anyone who entered the house, and it was often described as if you were in a vacuum. It was hard to breathe and as strange as it sounds, it often felt as if even gravity was stronger inside the house. There was also the spiritual aspect I can only describe as feeling like a constant attack to the core of my soul; I had horrible dreams of various demonic-looking characters attacking me and the other investigators.

All that aside, there were direct and relevant responses on various spirit boxes and other ITC devices. Several different types of video cameras were used in the house, including full spectrum and DVR cameras. The number of light anomalies captured was staggering. There were also countless light anomalies that were not captured on camera but were witnessed by various investigators. These manifestations included white and blue flashes of light and smoky mists that moved through the rooms.

One of the most significant aspects I noticed during and after the investigation, aside from the thousands of hours of video and audio documentation, is how each person involved was affected personally—

breakups and divorces, personality changes, financial problems, bad car wrecks, and even the loss of friends and family. It was uncanny how many negative things occurred during and after the investigation, even to those who weren't directly involved. I went to the Welles house to document supernatural occurrences. I got that and so much more. As my loving Mom always told me, "Be Careful what you ask for, son. You might just get it!"

It wasn't long after I returned home from my final investigation that I found myself at odds with Jerry. He was angry at my use of some of my personal footage caught during our investigation. We had a very bad falling out over the matter. On reflection, the fight shouldn't have been as bad as it was, but considering the darkness surrounding the house, I honestly wasn't too surprised at the developing friction. I'd seen a lot of friendships end during the course of the investigation. It's hard to say who or what was at fault. In my defense I just wanted to share my experience and my story of what I had dealt with and encountered, and how it affected my life.

Although I was done investigating the place, and safely away from it, things weren't easy at home. I was facing a bitter divorce. I had moved into a new house, and immediately began to experience unexplained noises. There were also loud popping sounds like those associated with reports of portals opening and closing. On a regular basis, I would see shadow movement out of the corners of my eyes. I also began to experience horrible nightmares on a frequent basis. This was not a problem I had ever experienced before, at least not until my time at the Welles house. There were unexplained voices coming from inside my new house, too, but they were difficult to distinguish or understand.

Two months after our falling out, Jerry called me out of the blue to see if I wanted to go back to the Welles house. Honestly, I couldn't believe what I was hearing. To think he had the gall to even ask me after the fight we'd had was unbelievable. I think maybe it was his way of trying to make amends, but there was no way in hell I was going back to that house.

I suffered a lot of loss as a result of my time investigating the Welles house and I have to wonder how many other people involved with the Welles investigations had to deal with unwanted attachments or negative influences. I continued to experience a string of problems

I attributed to spending so much time at the place. I was betrayed by someone I thought to be a true friend and had to sever those ties. I had financial difficulties, as well as several other minor things, but the run of bad luck seemed to go on and on, and I would soon take some more hits.

I was still having strange things happen at my new home. It all came to a head one night when I had a vision in my sleep that I was surrounded by this dark cloud, containing all these shadow-beings. They were reaching out and trying to pull me in with them, all the while telling me to kill myself. All I could do was pray, and as soon as I began praying, they were gone. The next night it happened again, but this time the dark cloud and shadow-beings were even closer to me. As they reached out for me, I could smell rotting flesh. Again, I began to pray and again, the creatures went away.

The next night was by far the worst. The cloud was really close this time, and the beings were making physical contact with me. They were ripping at my skin and making me bleed. They tore at my clothes and I could smell feces and rotting flesh all around me. I prayed, and it made the beings go away. When I woke up, I found I had several scratches on my arms and shoulders. I felt then and was firmly convinced, that the demons were a direct result of my time spent investigating the Welles house.

My run of bad luck seemed to stretch on. More friends I thought I could trust turned on me, and I experienced a lot of slander from people I thought were honest. I fully believed the evil from the Welles house was trying to attach itself to me and completely ruin my life.

I sought out a minister and he performed a cleansing on me. I felt better, but I wanted to go even further, so I sought out a Native American shaman and had him also do a cleansing, and even had a third one performed by a different priest. I didn't want to take any chances. Soon after the cleansing my luck began to change for the better. I started feeling healthy and happy. The lightness was returning. I continued my work in the paranormal, stronger, and better for all the darkness I had experienced. My name in the field was growing and I give credit for this to the true friends I have, as well as the fan base I've built along the way. I was reunited with my son's mom and I now have a new, beautiful daughter.

However, let my story serve as a warning to anyone who may

want to investigate highly negative locations. I went through a very real, personal hell and it was not a quick ordeal. It was one of the most negative periods in my life, and I know without a doubt it was largely due to so much time investigating the Welles house. It took more than a year before all the negativity was gone, and I wouldn't wish that grueling, unfortunate experience on anyone. Most people do not fully realize the dangers of investigating such locations. Take it from me, I've been there and lived it, and these types of places will affect your life. They should never be taken lightly.

    I made it out in one piece, and I tell this personal story so others can understand the dangers involved.

    Good luck and God speed to each and every one of you.

Aftermath

About the Authors

Dave Spinks

After experiencing an after-death visit from his grandfather, Dave Spinks became fascinated by the paranormal and started his search for answers. Gathering evidence in the form of EVPs, video and photographic data and personal experiences, Dave collected experiences from everyone he could and cites the television series "In Search Of" hosted by Leonard Nimoy as an early influence.

As an adult, he joined the USAF right out of college and became a trained observer. He spent nine years in the military, eight in the Air

About the Authors

Force and one in the Army National Guard in a Military Police unit.

After active duty, Dave pursued a career in law enforcement and studied criminal justice. He became a Federal Law Enforcement officer and spent eight years working for the US Department of Justice.

His professional path greatly enhanced his investigative experience. During his years working for the Government, he continued his pursuit of the paranormal and investigated every time he had an opportunity. His service gave him the chance to investigate international locations in Italy while stationed there in the 1990s.

In 2011, he retired from Law Enforcement and decided to pursue paranormal investigation on a full-time basis.

Since that time Dave has appeared on Numerous Television shows including Travel Channel's *These Woods are Haunted*, *Paranormal 911*, *Ghost Nation*, History Channel's *UnXplained*, Destination America's *Terror in the Woods* and Discovery Network's *Expedition X*. Dave also appeared in the documentary *The Flatwoods Monster, a Legacy of Fear*.

He is a featured guest speaker at Paranormal conferences around the country and a featured guest on numerous podcasts and radio broadcasts around the world. Dave has also authored books on hauntings, cryptids, and UFOs.

"I like to share what I do with others, in the hopes of answering some of man's greatest questions: Is there life after death? Are there unknown creatures walking among us? Are we alone in the universe? I believe we are not alone, and finding answers is my motivation."

Learn more about Dave Spinks and the investigation at the Welles house online at:

http://www.davespinksparanormalinvestigator.com/

David Weatherly

David Weatherly is a renaissance man of the strange and supernatural. He has traveled the world in pursuit of ghosts, cryptids, UFOs, magic, and more. From the specters of dusty castles, to remote, haunted islands, from ancient sites, to modern mysteries, he has journeyed to the most unusual places on the globe seeking the unknown.

David became fascinated with the paranormal at a young age. Ghost stories and accounts of weird creatures and UFOs led him

About the Authors

to discover many of his early influences. Writers such as John Keel, Jacques Vallee, Hans Holzer and others set him on course to spend his life exploring and investigating the unexplained.

Throughout his life, he's also delved into shamanic and magical traditions from around the world, spending time with elders from numerous cultures in Europe, the Americas, Africa and Asia. He has studied with Taoist masters in China, Tibetan Lamas, and other mystics from the far east. He's picked up knowledge from African and Native American tribal elders and sat around fires with shamans from countless other traditions.

Along his path, David has also gathered a lot of arcane knowledge, studying a range of ancient arts from palmistry, the runes, and other obscure forms of divination, to alchemy and magick. He has studied and taught Qigong and Ninjutsu, as well as various energy related arts. David has also studied stage and performance magic.

His shamanic and magical background has given him a unique perspective in his explorations into the unknown, and he continues to write, travel and explore, leaving no stone unturned in his quest for the strange and unusual.

David has investigated, and written about, a diverse range of topics including, Hauntings & Ghosts, Cryptozoology, Ufology, Ancient Mysteries, Shamanism, Magic, and Psychic Phenomena.

David is the founder of the independent media and publishing company, Eerie Lights Publishing.

He has been a featured speaker at conferences around the world and has lectured for countless paranormal and spiritual groups.

He is a frequent guest on Coast to Coast AM with George Noory, Spaced Out Radio and other radio programs. David has also appeared on numerous television shows including the Travel Channel's Mysteries of the Outdoors, History Channel's Ancient Aliens, Beyond Belief and other programs. He was also featured in the highly successful series On the Trail of UFOs.

David's books include Strange Intruders, Eerie Companions, and the Cryptid States series.

Find David online at:

Eerielights.com

Made in the USA
Middletown, DE
02 November 2025